THE SHIFT

THE SHIFT

REWIRE YOUR BODY.
RECLAIM YOUR MIND.
RESTORE YOUR LIFE.

TIMOTHY ELDRED

For permission requests, contact: admin@1to1solutions.com

Publisher: 1:1 Solutions Group, LLC.

ISBN: 979-8-9944468-6-7

This book is a work of nonfiction. The stories and examples throughout are drawn from real patterns I've observed in my own life and in the lives of people I've encountered over decades. Some names and identifying details have been changed to protect privacy. The content is based on personal experience and research but is not a substitute for professional medical, psychological, or legal advice. Always consult a qualified professional for advice related to your specific circumstances.

Printed in the United States of America

Contents

Preface

This book isn't meant to be skimmed. It's meant to be lived. Don't read it to finish—it's not a race. Read it to feel. Pause when something hits. Reread when something resonates.

Take your time. Try the practices. Let your body, mind, and spirit catch up.

There's no pressure to get it perfect. Just an invitation to come home to the version of you that's been waiting.

The shift begins the moment you decide to stop surviving and start showing up as the real you.

So, if you're still reading? You've already started.

INTRODUCTION

I came home early. Again. Another day of sitting at my desk like a zombie, staring at the screen, getting nothing done. Another day in the liminal—the in-between. Another day waiting for the meds to do their job.

The medication that was supposed to manage the disorder came with its own prison. Fogginess. Confusion. Depression. I could live in chronic pain and not be able to think. Or I could take the meds, be pain-free, and still not be able to think.

Either way, my mind was mush.

Cindy was already in the pool when I got home. "It's hot," she called out. "Put on your suit. Come cool off with me."

I didn't care. But it was hot. So I did.

I walked out to our patio. Cindy was in the water, looking at me expectantly. And I froze.

I stood at the edge. But I didn't know what to do. I couldn't remember how to get in the pool. Seriously. I couldn't.

My body wouldn't move. My brain wouldn't tell it how. I just stood there, frozen, staring at water I'd climbed into a thousand times before. Step over. That's all I had to do. One foot, then the other. But the signal from my brain to my legs was gone. Like someone had cut the wire.

"What are you doing?" Cindy asked. "Get in the pool."

I opened my mouth to answer, and nothing came out. I didn't know what I was doing. I didn't know why I couldn't move. I didn't know anything anymore.

"I don't know," I finally said. "I don't know."

And then something broke.

Not quietly. Not gracefully. I started sobbing—the kind of sobbing that comes from somewhere deeper than grief. The kind that buckles your knees and steals your breath. I stood there at the edge of my own pool, fifty years old, shaking and crying and completely lost. Not lost like you lose your keys. Lost like you lose yourself. Like you wake up one day and the person you thought you were is just... gone.

I couldn't get in the water. I couldn't stop crying. I couldn't explain what was happening because I didn't understand it myself. My mind was gone. Either the pain had destroyed my ability to think, or the medication had. There was no third option. No escape route. No way out.

Eventually, somehow, I threw my leg over the side and stepped into the water. I sank slowly, and Cindy held me. She didn't try to fix it. She couldn't. Nobody could.

This wasn't new. It had been building for months.

In 2020, I got blindsided by a diagnosis I couldn't even pronounce. Glossopharyngeal neuralgia—a nerve disorder so rare most doctors will never see a case. And ruthless. Electric shocks firing through my throat, my ear, my jaw with every swallow, every yawn, every sneeze, every moment of existence. No trigger. No warning. Like being stabbed in the skull with a pitchfork on repeat.

Every. Damn. Day.

But that wasn't the end of it.

During one of the endless scans, the doctors found something else. A 9mm aneurysm, buried like a ticking time bomb in my intracranial carotid artery. I sat there with Cindy, staring at a surgeon in a lab coat as he looked me in the eye and said, "Sign your advance directives. Get your affairs in order."

Not figuratively. Not gently. As a matter of fact. Word for word.

At that moment, I didn't feel brave. I felt erased. Like the man I'd worked my whole life to become had just been crossed out in front of me.

The aneurysm didn't rupture. It's still there. A silent reminder that life is fragile. A gift to stop wasting time proving I'm okay.

But the pain wasn't done with me yet.

The meds they gave me to manage the nerve disorder hijacked my mind. The fog settled in so deep I couldn't be left alone. Friends had to sit with me during the day while Cindy was at work to make sure I didn't do something permanent.

We even had the conversation I wouldn't wish on anyone— do we need to get the guns out of the house?

So hear me when I say this clearly. I know why people take their own lives. It's not selfish. It's survival when you can't trust your own mind to stay in the fight.

That night, after the pool, I sat on the edge of the bed. Cindy sat next to me. She didn't say anything at first. She just waited.

"I don't want to do this anymore," I finally admitted.

She didn't flinch. She looked at me with eyes that held something I hadn't expected—not fear, but recognition.

"I've been watching you disappear for months," she said. "The Tim I married used to fill a room. Now you barely take up space in it."

That was the moment that stripped me bare. No more posturing. No more pretending. Just one brutal question echoing in the dark: Am I actually living my life or surviving the one I built?

I knew all the right answers. I'd spent decades on stages giving them to other people. But knowing something and living it are two different things. And the gap between what I learned and what I felt had become a canyon I couldn't cross.

My mind was full of truth. My body was full of terror. And no amount of thinking could close that distance.

What I didn't understand back then is that survival mode didn't start with pain. It started with programming.

It wasn't one bad habit. It wasn't even a packed schedule. It was the systems that shaped me. School taught me to perform.

Church taught me to behave. Culture taught me to grind. And somewhere along the way, I lost myself.

Not all at once. Or with a breakdown. Slowly. Quietly. Over time. Trading presence for pressure. Peace for applause. Self-trust for the approval of systems that never cared who I really was anyway.

The world didn't break me with demands. It broke me with its definitions of success, worth, and what it means to be "enough."

And here's what's crazy:

We actually applaud what destroys us. Call exhaustion dedication. Even confuse being needed with being loved.

I'd been doing this for decades. Stages. Pulpits. Boardrooms. I was good at it. I could hold an audience. I knew how to smile when everything inside me was collapsing. How to land the line at just the right moment and make everyone believe I had it figured out.

But my body knew better. It was finished. And I was undone. No title. No stage. No strategy could save me. Because I wasn't just burned out. I was burned through.

So I stopped pretending.

I stopped trying to fix myself with more of what had broken me. I let go of everything I thought I knew. And I traded the grind for the ground beneath my feet. Something solid and more humane.

What I found wasn't a new identity. It was my true one. I didn't just heal. I became whole.

The emptiness I'd carried for years wasn't a flaw to hide. It was a signal to listen to. The shift wasn't about filling my void with more achievement or approval. It was about finally standing still long enough to hear what it had been trying to tell me all along.

You can't *think* your way out of a body stuck in survival mode. You have to *feel* your way back to life.

And what I discovered wasn't hype, hustle, or spiritual shortcuts. It was hidden in the intersection of science and stillness. Breathwork and biology. Ancient rhythms backed by modern research. I started rewiring my body—not with willpower, but with light and breath. Cold water and rhythm. In time, my mind followed. And piece by piece, I redesigned my life—from the inside out.

Here's what nobody tells you about transformation: The systems that broke you count on your silence. They bet you'll apply what you've learned quietly and call it "self-care" or "personal growth" without naming the truth. That we're living in structures designed for productivity, not humanity.

Your breakdown wasn't a personal failure. It was a sane response to insane expectations.

What if your body's collapse wasn't weakness, but wisdom—the final desperate attempt to communicate what your conditioned mind couldn't yet see?

This book isn't about tweaking your morning routine or finding five steps to better balance. It's about fundamental liberation from systems never designed for you to thrive. It's about recognizing the path to freedom doesn't begin with more effort. It begins with a different truth.

Not the truth of burnout culture, performance addiction, or corporate systems that mine your life for productivity. But the truth of your biology. Your nervous system. Your divine design.

The truth your body has been trying to tell you all along—if you'd only stop long enough to listen.

This book is the result of that journey.

I've done the hard work and heavy lifting for you—from reading and researching to testing and teaching. These pages hold the distilled essence of everything I've lived through, fought for, and found over the last few years.

They're for people who've hit the wall and are done pretending everything's fine. People like me. People like you.

You don't need hype. You need hope that actually works. You don't need another breakthrough moment. You need a rhythm you can live with. You don't need to become someone else. You just need to embrace who you already are—your authentic self.

This isn't a motivational book. It's a field guide for collapse and a breath map for coming back to life. What you'll find here isn't self-help. It's self-restoration. It's not about doing more. It's about becoming whole.

The framework in this book follows five movements. I call them The S.H.I.F.T.—and each letter represents a stage of the journey from surviving to actually living.

S — Safety First. Transformation doesn't begin with strategy—it begins when your body finally believes it's safe enough to change. This is the foundation everything else is built on. Skip it, and nothing else holds.

H — Heal the Story. You're not living your life—you're living a story someone else wrote. The loops running in your head aren't truth—they're code. Scripts you inherited or invented to survive.

I — Integrate the Whole. Body, mind, and spirit aren't separate systems to manage. They're one ecosystem. Healing means learning to align them instead of fragmenting yourself to fit into broken systems.

F — Form New Rhythms. Breakthroughs open doors—rhythms keep you walking through them. Freedom without structure is chaos. This is where you build containers that make transformation sustainable.

T — Transform Your World. You don't need to escape your life—you need to build one you can stay inside. This isn't about becoming someone different. It's about returning to the person you've always been.

Each chapter will take you deeper. Each chapter will give you something real to practice—not just ideas to think about. By the time you finish, you won't just understand the shift. You'll be living it.

This book blends biology with spirit. Practical science with sacred rhythm. And it's built for the version of you who's exhausted from trying everything else.

I'm not going to sell you a fantasy. I'm going to show you a path—one I walked myself when I had nothing left to lose. It's not glamorous. It's not always easy. But it's real. And it works.

The shift begins the moment you decide to stop surviving and start showing up as the real you.

Let's go.

— S —

Safety First

Your body must believe before your mind can change.

You can't change your life from the neck *up*. I know. I tried for years. I read every book on transformation I could find. Underlined passages until my highlighters ran dry. Filled journals with insights. Set goals with deadlines and accountability systems that would make a project manager weep with joy. I crafted mission statements so clear I could see them in my sleep. I memorized affirmations until they played on loop in my subconscious. I practiced gratitude until my hand cramped from writing.

I was a professional at change—on stage, teaching others how to transform their lives. I had the frameworks, the theology, the neuroscience, the principles. I could stand before a thousand people and deliver a message that moved them to tears.

People flew me across the country for coaching. Organizations paid top dollar for my insights.

And every morning, I woke up with my heart pounding, my stomach in knots, dreading a day that hadn't even begun.

My mind was full of truth. My body was full of terror. But I couldn't think my way out of that gap.

I'd lie in bed at 3am, quoting Scripture about peace without being able to drown out the doubts I was thinking. I'd try to "be still and know" while grinding my teeth hard enough to crack a crown. I'd journal about surrender while holding my breath without even realizing it.

Here's the line I wish someone had tattooed on my forehead for me to see in the mirror every day:

Your body doesn't care what you believe.
It only responds to what it feels.

The gap between what I believed and what I experienced became a chasm. A chasm that swallowed my confidence, my health, and nearly my sanity.

What I didn't understand—what no one had told me—was that I was trying to build a house on quicksand. I was working on the roof when there was no foundation. I was installing windows when the walls hadn't been framed.

I was trying to transform my life while my nervous system was waging a war that had already ended.

The Intelligence You've Been Ignoring

Here's what no one told me—what most transformation programs don't acknowledge, what even therapy often misses:

Your body has its own intelligence. And that intelligence doesn't care about your goals, your beliefs, or your good intentions.

It only cares about one thing: *survival.*

Dr. Stephen Porges, the neuroscientist whose work revolutionized our understanding of the nervous system, introduced a concept that changed everything for me: neuroception. It's your body's unconscious threat-detection system. Not your brain's conscious analysis of danger—your body's automatic, below-awareness scanning for safety or threat.

It's running right now. This very moment. While you read these words. It's assessing your environment, your internal state, your breathing patterns, the sounds around you, the tension in your muscles. It's making calculations you'll never consciously access.

And here's the problem that defines modern existence: your nervous system can't tell the difference between a hungry lion and a demanding boss. Between a life-threatening attack and an overflowing inbox. Between mortal danger and modern life.

It responds the same way to all of it.

Fight. Flight. Freeze.

When your body thinks you're in danger—real or not—it doesn't ask questions. It reacts. Cortisol floods. Adrenaline spikes. Your heart pounds. Everything not essential to survival shuts down. Digestion shuts down—no time to process food when you're about to be someone's lunch. As your muscles tighten, your breath goes shallow and rapid, efficient for sprinting but devastating for thinking.

And your prefrontal cortex—the part of your brain responsible for planning, deciding, regulating emotion, and seeing the big picture—gets fuzzy. Resources get redirected to survival structures. Because survival doesn't need creativity. Survival doesn't need nuance. Survival needs reaction.

This is brilliant design when you're facing an actual emergency. Run from the lion. Fight off the attacker. Freeze so the predator doesn't see you. Survive now, process later.

It's catastrophic design when the emergency never ends.

Your nervous system evolved over millennia for a very specific type of stress: immediate, resolvable, physical threats. See lion. Run from lion. Survive lion. Return to baseline. Rest. Recover. Eat. Connect with tribe. Sleep under stars. Repeat to live another day.

The stress response was designed to be acute. Intense but brief. A sprint, not a marathon. Your ancestors faced maybe a handful of genuine survival threats in a year. The rest of the time, their nervous systems could return to a state of rest and restoration.

But modern life has no baseline. The lion is everywhere.

The lion is in your pocket, buzzing with notifications at 11pm.

The lion is in your inbox, multiplying while you sleep.

The lion is in the 24-hour news cycle, feeding you a continuous stream of things to fear.

The lion is in social media, showing you everyone who's doing better than you.

The lion is in the economy, the political climate, the cultural chaos, the uncertainty of everything you thought was stable.

The lion is in the expectations you carry—from your boss, your family, your religion, your culture, your own inner critic who's never satisfied no matter how much you accomplish.

And because the threat never resolves, your nervous system never returns to rest. Survival mode becomes your permanent state of being. Fight-or-flight becomes your baseline. The emergency state designed to last minutes now lasts years.

The numbers are staggering. The American Institute of Stress reports that 77% of Americans regularly experience physical symptoms caused by stress. Anxiety disorders affect 40 million adults. Burnout has been officially classified as an occupational phenomenon by the World Health Organization.

We're not experiencing an epidemic of character weakness. We're experiencing a species-wide mismatch between the bodies we inherited and the world we've built.

You're not tired because you're lazy.

You're not anxious because you lack faith.

You're not foggy because you're undisciplined.

You're dysregulated.

Your nervous system is stuck watching reruns of Survivor and no amount of willpower, mindset work, or spiritual striving can override the body's most primal programming. You can't outthink your wiring.

People Like You

I lived in this state for years without naming it.

I called it being committed. Being responsible. Taking my work seriously. I wore stress like a badge of honor. I thought the fact that I couldn't turn my mind off meant I was more called or cared more than other people. I thought my intensity and passion were dedication.

But my body was telling a different story.

My heart would race before I even got out of bed. My palms would sweat in normal conversations. I could hear my own blood pressure pounding in my ears.

I'd check my email the moment I woke up—before my feet hit the floor, before I'd said good morning to Cindy—and the racing would get worse as the notifications loaded. Not because anything was actually urgent. *Because my body had learned that everything was urgent.* Every message could be a threat. Every notification was a crisis to manage.

Picture a VP of operations at a logistics company. Need a department problem solved? Call him. He's steady, reliable, unflappable—at work anyway. But at home? He can't sit through a family dinner without checking his phone. His wife says his mind is "always somewhere else." Over the last three years, he's gained forty pounds, and he can't remember the last time he slept through the night without Lunesta. He needs two bourbons just to quiet his brain enough to watch TV. He's not living. He's barely managing.

Now, picture a social worker with fifteen years in child protective services. She's seen things that would break most people. She tells herself she's fine—she has to be fine, because other people need her to be fine. But her body keeps score. Chronic migraines. Digestive issues no doctor can explain. A startle response so sensitive that her own kids know not to surprise her. She cries in her car before walking into work, composes herself, does her job, then cries again on the way home. She calls it "just the job." It's actually her nervous system screaming for relief that never comes.

Now, picture a pastor of a growing church. Everyone sees the man on stage—confident, articulate, spiritually grounded. But no one sees the man who wakes at 4am with his heart racing, worrying he said something wrong in last week's sermon. No one sees the person—not the pastor—who needs three cups of coffee just to function, who snaps at his wife over nothing, who sits in his office some afternoons unable to form a coherent thought. He preaches about the peace of God while his body lives in perpetual war.

Now, picture a mother of three who hasn't had a full night's sleep in seven years. Not because of the kids. They sleep fine now. Because her brain won't stop running scenarios. What if the kids get sick? What if the money runs out? What if something happens to her partner? What if she's failing at everything and everyone's just too nice to tell her? She scrolls her phone until her eyes can't stay open. Too wired to sleep. Too exhausted to do anything productive. She'd describe herself as "just tired." She's actually living in a never-ending low-grade panic attack.

Different lives. Different responsibilities. Same underlying reality.

Their bodies have been hijacked by a nervous system stuck in emergency mode. And no amount of trying harder, believing more, or pushing through is going to fix it.

Because you can't think your way out of a body braced for catastrophe.

THE SCIENCE THAT CHANGES EVERYTHING

Here's the principle that rewired my entire approach to transformation: SAFETY BEFORE STRATEGY.

You cannot build sustainable change on a dysregulated nervous system. Period. All the goal-setting, habit-stacking, mindset-shifting, and motivational strategies in the world will fail if your body doesn't believe it's safe enough to change.

Think about it: change is inherently destabilizing. New behaviors feel unfamiliar. Unfamiliar feels threatening. Threatening triggers survival mode. Survival mode shuts down the very brain regions you need to learn, adapt, and grow.

This is why New Year's resolutions fail by February. Why you can read a book that changes your perspective—and nothing actually changes in your life. Why you can have profound

insights in therapy, at a retreat, or sitting through a sermon—
and still find yourself stuck in the same patterns a month later.

Insight without safety is just information. And information
isn't transformation.

Your nervous system needs to believe the new behavior is
safe before it will allow you to sustain it.

This is revolutionary because it flips the entire transformation industry on its head. We've been taught that change starts
with the mind—with belief, decision, willpower. That's bullshit.
Because neuroscience says otherwise. Change that sticks starts
with the body—with a nervous system that feels secure enough
to let go of old survival strategies.

Dr. Bessel van der Kolk, whose work with trauma survivors
has transformed our understanding of the body-mind connection, puts it bluntly: "The body keeps the score." Your nervous
system remembers every moment of overwhelm, every threat
your conscious mind has forgotten. And it runs defensive programs based on that memory—whether you want it to or not.

The path forward isn't to override your body with your will.
It's to partner with your body by giving it what it needs to feel
safe.

Only then can real change begin.

The Nervous System Reset

The practices that follow aren't random wellness tips.
They're a systematic approach to resetting your nervous system

from survival mode to safety mode—what I call THE NERVOUS SYSTEM RESET.

Each practice targets a specific part of your body's threat-detection system. Together, they send one message to your nervous system: The emergency is over. You can stand down. It's safe to heal now.

They work because they bypass the thinking brain entirely. You can't reason your way into regulation. But you can signal your way there—through sun, breath, movement, temperature, and rhythm.

These aren't things you should do. They're things that work.

The difference matters. I'm not giving you a guilt-inducing list of pie-in-the-sky practices. I'm giving you a toolkit that directly addresses the physiological roots of your struggle.

Chapter by chapter, we build. But we start with the body.

PRACTICE 1: MORNING LIGHT PROTOCOL

What: Get direct sunlight exposure within 30-60 minutes of waking. 10-15 minutes minimum on clear days, 20-30 minutes on cloudy days. (Geography and climate can be challenging. But don't make it your excuse.)

Why it works: Light entering your eyes triggers hormonal signals that set your circadian rhythm—the master clock that regulates everything from cortisol to melatonin. When you miss morning light, your body never gets the signal that day has begun. Your stress hormones don't peak when they should (morning), which means they stay elevated when they shouldn't (evening). This simple disruption creates downstream chaos in mood, energy, sleep, and stress resilience.

Dr. Andrew Huberman's research at Stanford has shown that morning light exposure is one of the single most powerful tools for regulating the nervous system. It doesn't just affect your sleep—it affects your entire stress response architecture.

How to do it—exactly:

First thing when you wake up: Get outside. Not through a window—glass filters out the specific wavelengths you need. Not on your porch with sunglasses—you need light hitting your retinas directly.

If it's cloudy: Stay out a little longer. Cloudy skies still provide 10,000+ lux, but you need more exposure time.

If it's still dark when you wake: Use a 10,000 lux therapy lamp for 20-30 minutes while you do your morning routine.

Combine it with something you already do: Take your coffee outside. Walk to the end of your driveway to get the mail. Stand on your porch while you check your phone (if you must check it).

Don't make it complicated: You're not training for a marathon. You're standing in light. Sixty seconds is better than zero. Build from there.

What happens in your body: Cortisol spikes appropriately in the morning (this is good—it's your "wake up and be alert" signal). This early spike means cortisol will drop appropriately in the evening. Melatonin production gets properly suppressed, then rebounds at night when you need it. Your hormones start working together again.

What you'll notice: Better energy in the morning. Less afternoon crash. Easier time falling asleep at night. Over time, you'll wake more naturally—less dependent on alarm clocks and caffeine to kick your day in the butt.

PRACTICE 2: PROTEIN-FIRST BREAKFAST

What: Eat 30+ grams of protein within an hour of waking. Before carbs. And before caffeine (ideally).

Why it works: Blood sugar stability is directly linked to nervous system regulation. When blood sugar spikes and crashes, your body reads it as a threat—releasing cortisol and adrenaline to compensate. The standard American breakfast (toast, cereal, juice, muffins) is essentially a blood sugar bomb that sets you up for a mid-morning crash, which your body interprets as an emergency.

Protein, on the other hand, provides stable, slow-release energy that keeps blood sugar even. When blood sugar is stable, your nervous system can relax. There's no emergency to respond to.

How to do it—exactly:

Before anything else: A glass of water. You're dehydrated from sleep. Hydrate before you caffeinate.

The minimum effective dose: 4 eggs (28g protein). Scrambled, fried, poached—however you'll actually eat them. 10 minutes.

If you hate cooking in the morning: Pre-cook egg muffins on Sunday (12 eggs, baked in a muffin tin = grab-and-go protein for the week). Or: a quality protein shake with collagen powder. Or: full-fat Greek yogurt (20g protein per cup) with fruit and nuts.

If you're not hungry in the morning: That's the dysregulation talking. Start small—a handful of almonds and a hard-boiled egg. Your appetite will come back as your system settles.

The order matters: Protein and fat first. Carbs after—if you want them. Eating in this order keeps your blood sugar from spiking.

Caffeine note: Coffee on an empty stomach jacks up your cortisol when it's already high. Eat first. Or at least eat with it.

What happens in your body: Blood sugar stays steady instead of spiking and crashing. Cortisol does what it's supposed to do.

What you'll notice: No mid-morning crash. Clearer thinking. Less anxiety. You'll stop reaching for that 10am snack or your third cup of coffee.

PRACTICE 3: COLD EXPOSURE PROTOCOL

What: End your shower with 30-60 seconds of cold water. As cold as it goes.

Why it works: This is controlled stress—a brief, intense challenge that your body learns to handle. Unlike chronic stress (which never resolves), cold exposure has a clear beginning and end. Your body experiences the stress, adapts to it, then returns to baseline.

This trains your nervous system that not all stress is dangerous. It builds what researchers call "stress inoculation"—the capacity to face challenge without getting stuck in panic mode.

Exposure to cold also triggers a massive release of norepinephrine—a neurotransmitter that improves focus, mood, and resilience. Studies show increases of 200-300% from cold water immersion.

How to do it—exactly:

Start ridiculously small: The last 15 seconds of your shower, turn it to cold. Not lukewarm—cold. Yes, you will hate it. That's the point.

Build incrementally: After a week, go to 30 seconds. After two weeks, 45 seconds. Work up to 60-90 seconds over a month.

Breathe through it: Your first instinct will be to hold your breath. Don't. Slow, controlled breathing through the cold is part of the training—it teaches your nervous system to stay regulated under stress.

The shock is the medicine: If it doesn't make you gasp and cuss a little, it's not cold enough. Your body needs that jolt—and then the recovery. That's the rewiring.

What happens in your body: Norepinephrine spikes, which sharpens your focus and lifts your mood. Circulation improves. Your cortisol spikes too—but then it actually comes back down, which is the whole point. You're training your system to handle stress and recover from it.

What you'll notice: Mental clarity after the shower. Elevated mood. A sense of having handled something hard before 8am. Over time, you'll notice things that used to spike your anxiety just don't hit as hard.

PRACTICE 4: SHUTDOWN RITUAL

What: A consistent 30-60 minute wind-down routine that signals to your body: the day is over.

Why it works: Your nervous system doesn't have a clear boundary between "on" and "off" unless you create one. In a world of 24/7 access, your threat-detection system never gets the signal that it's safe to stand down.

A shutdown ritual is that signal. It's a consistent, predictable sequence that your body learns to associate with safety and rest.

How to do it—exactly:

Set a hard stop: Pick a time when work ends. For me, it's around 8pm. After that—no email, no texts, no "just one more thing." Non-negotiable.

Screens off: At least 30 minutes before bed, screens go off or switch to night mode. Blue light tells your brain it's still daytime. I've set my phone to use red light automatically at 8pm.

Change the environment: Dim the lights. Light a candle if that's your thing. Put on your "soft clothes," as I call mine. Your body learns to pick up on these subtle clues—give it a hint.

Wind down: Do something that shifts you from doing to being. Stretch a little. Read some fiction. Sit outside on your deck. Talk to someone you love about something that isn't a problem.

Gratitude—keep it simple: Write down three things that went well today. Not a journal entry. Just three things to train your brain to look for good instead of threat. I reflect on the intention I set for myself in the morning.

Same bedtime: Your body wants rhythm. Hit the pillow within the same 30-minute window every night. And yes, weekends too.

What happens in your body: Cortisol drops as your system recognizes the "day is done" signal. Melatonin rises in the dimmed lighting. Nervous system shifts from sympathetic (activated) to parasympathetic (rest and digest). Brain waves slow toward sleep-ready patterns.

What you'll notice: Faster sleep onset. Fewer racing thoughts. Waking more rested. Over time, you'll start naturally getting tired at your target bedtime—your body will anticipate rest and prepare for it.

PRACTICE 5: THE TWO-MINUTE RESET

What: A rapid nervous system regulation technique you can use anytime you feel activated—in a meeting, in traffic, in a conflict, in a moment of overwhelm.

Why it works: Your breath is the only autonomic function you can consciously control. By deliberately shifting your breathing pattern, you directly influence your nervous system state. Slow, controlled exhalations activate the parasympathetic nervous system (rest and digest) and signal safety.

This practice gives you a tool that works in seconds—not hours, not days. When you feel yourself getting hijacked by stress, you can intervene immediately.

How to do it—exactly:

The pattern: Inhale 4 seconds. Hold 2. Exhale 6. Hold 2. Repeat 4-6 times. The longer exhale is what activates the calming response.

The key is the exhale: Longer exhales activate the vagus nerve and shift you toward parasympathetic dominance. The longer your exhale relative to your inhale, the stronger the calming signal.

Where to use it: Before walking into a difficult meeting. When you feel your chest tightening in traffic. When your partner says something that triggers you. When your kid pushes your buttons. Before opening your email. After hanging up a frustrating phone call.

Nobody has to know: You can do this anywhere—at your desk, on the toilet, in your car. No one can tell you're doing nervous system regulation. It just looks like you're pausing.

What happens in your body: Heart rate decreases. Blood pressure drops. Vagus nerve activates. Prefrontal cortex comes back online (you can think clearly again). Stress hormones begin to clear.

What you'll notice: Immediate calming effect. More space between stimulus and response. The ability to choose your reaction instead of being hijacked by it. Over time, you'll need fewer resets. Calm becomes your default.

THE SACRED DIMENSION

For those with eyes to see it, nervous system regulation isn't just health practice. It's spiritual discipline.

Scripture speaks of a God who knit us together—body, mind, and spirit woven as one from the very first moment.

Your body is the first gift you were given. The first medium through which you experience love, beauty, connection, and purpose. It's not a container for your soul—it's an expression of it. Not a prison—a partner.

For decades, I treated my body as a tool to be used for spiritual work. I fasted regularly—not for spiritual clarity but as punishment. I pushed through exhaustion as proof of devotion. I ignored pain as evidence of my commitment. All in the name of faith.

But true devotion includes tending to the gift. Not abusing it.

When you honor your body—when you give it light and rest and nourishment and care—you're not being selfish. You're being sacred. You're stewarding the first and most intimate gift you were ever given.

The ancient practices understood this. Breath awareness in prayer traditions. Physical preparation for worship. Sabbath rest not as optional but as commandment. Fasting—not as punishment but as reset, as creating space for something else to fill.

These weren't arbitrary rituals invented by people who didn't understand science. They were recognition that the body and the spirit speak the same language. That you can't have one without the other. That what happens in the physical affects the spiritual—and what moves in the spiritual shows up in the physical.

Every intentional breath is a prayer.
Every grounding movement is worship.
Every restored rhythm is an act of faith.

Before and After: What Changes

Before regulation, you live on edge.

You wake up with your heart already pounding. Small stuff feels like big stuff—someone cuts you off in traffic and it ruins your whole morning. Emotions hit hard, then go numb when there's too much to feel. Your body holds tension you don't even notice until you try to relax and realize you don't know how. You don't rest at the end of the day—you collapse. Sleep comes, but you wake up just as tired as when you went to bed.

I lived this way for so long I thought it was normal. I didn't even know there was an alternative. I thought everyone had a constant undercurrent of dread. I thought jumping at noises and bracing for impact was just what responsible adults did. I thought the tightness in my chest was just... how life felt.

After regulation becomes your new normal, everything shifts.

Not overnight—this isn't a pill that takes effect in thirty minutes. But gradually. Incrementally. In ways you almost don't notice until you look back at where you were.

You wake with presence instead of panic. There's space between stimulus and response. Challenges come, and you respond with clarity instead of reactivity. Emotions move through you without body-slamming you—you can feel sad without drowning, angry without exploding.

Your body holds less chronic tension. You realize your shoulders can exist somewhere other than next to your ears. Your breath deepens naturally, without you forcing it. Your jaw unclenches. Brow unfurls.

The shift accumulates. Moments of unexpected calm that slowly expand. One morning you realize you went a whole day without that familiar pit in your stomach. Then a week. Then you start to forget what it felt like—that constant hum of anxiety that used to be background noise.

For me, one of the first signs was realizing I'd gone an entire day without scanning for the nearest exit—a habit I'd developed during the worst of my health crisis. I'd walk into a room and immediately look for a way out.

Physical changes come alongside emotional ones. Digestion improves—your gut and your nervous system are intimately connected. Sleep deepens. Energy stabilizes. The fog lifts. And connection feels safer.

Not because the world changed. Because your body finally stopped sounding the alarm.

Remember that VP of operations? Two months into morning light and shutdown rituals, his wife said something he wasn't expecting: "You're actually here." He'd dropped fifteen pounds without trying. His body wasn't holding fat for survival anymore. He still checks his phone too much—but now it's a choice.

That social worker? Her migraines cut in half after six weeks. She still does hard work. Still sees the worst-case scenario sometimes. But it's not living in her body now. Her kids even told her she laughs more. She hadn't even noticed.

That pastor? He still wakes up early—but not in panic. Cold showers and protein-first mornings became non-negotiable. The racing thoughts quieted down. He preaches the same sermons. But now, he truly believes them.

And that mother who couldn't sleep? The shutdown ritual changed everything. Screens off at 9pm. Three gratitudes before bed. Same sleep time every night. Within a month, she was sleeping through the night for the first time in six years. She describes it simply: "I got my brain back."

THE RESISTANCE YOU'LL FACE

This path isn't without obstacles. Naming them now will help you navigate them without quitting.

Our economy runs on anxiety. Our media profits from outrage. Our workplaces reward chronic stress and call it dedication. When you start prioritizing regulation, you'll face pushback—from your boss, your colleagues, maybe even your family. You'll be accused of slacking off, checking out, not being a team player.

I lost opportunities when I stopped being available 24/7. Some people interpreted my boundaries as lack of commitment. A few relationships didn't survive my changes. The systems that needed my constant availability didn't quietly accept my new limits.

Expect this. Plan for it. And remember that the system's resistance is not evidence that you're wrong—it's evidence that you're changing.

As your body settles, emotions you've suppressed may surface. Grief. Anger. Fear. Sadness you've been running from for years. All the feelings you shoved down because there was no safe place to feel them.

About six weeks into my regulation practice, I experienced unexpected waves of grief. Not just about my health challenges—but about years of ignoring my body's signals. Years of treating myself like a machine. A lifetime of deferred feeling finally demanding its due. The discoveries were amazing because they were brand new for me.

This isn't regression. It's integration. Your body finally feels safe enough to process what it's been holding. Let it come. Let it move through you. This is part of the healing.

Genuine emergencies will come. High-demand seasons will hit. A parent will get sick. A job will be lost. A crisis will demand everything you have. And in those moments, your regulated practices will feel like luxuries you can't afford.

Don't believe that lie.

Crisis is precisely when regulation matters most. Not as a luxury—as a lifeline.

The Mantra

You don't need motivation. You need regulation.

Write it down. Stick it on your mirror. Make it your phone's screensaver. Put it someplace you can't miss it.

This is where the shift begins. Not with bigger goals or more willpower. Not with better beliefs or stronger faith. It starts when your body finally catches up to what your mind already knows:

You're safe. You can handle this. You're not stuck.

Reflection Questions

1. When during your day do you feel most dysregulated? What environmental or situational triggers seem to activate your survival response?

2. Which of the five practices resonates most strongly with where you are right now? What would it look like to commit to just that one practice for the next seven days?

3. If your body could speak directly to you, what would it say it needs most right now for safety?

THE INVITATION

This is where it starts. No big moment required. Just your body learning it's safe enough to change.

Everything else builds from here. But nothing works until your nervous system gets the message: the war is over.

Tomorrow morning, go outside. Light in your eyes. Feet on the ground. One breath that actually fills your lungs.

Then tell yourself what you need to hear:

You're safe now. *We're going to be okay.*

That's the first shift. It changes everything.

Continue the practice. Scan for the free daily companion app.

— **H** —

HEAL THE STORY

Rewrite the loop. Or it rewrites you.

The voice showed up around 6am. I was three weeks into my regulation practice. The morning panic had loosened. My energy was stabilizing.

For the first time in months, I was waking up without my heart already racing. The cold showers were working. The morning light was working. My nervous system was starting to believe—maybe—that survival mode wasn't the only option.

And that's when I heard it. Clear as a bell, like someone was standing in the room with me.

You're only valuable when you're producing.

I sat up in bed. Looked around. Cindy was still asleep, her breathing slow and steady. The house was quiet. Dawn was just beginning to lighten the edges of the blinds. But that sentence hung in the air like it had been spoken aloud.

It wasn't new. That thought had been running in my head for as long as I could remember. In the background, but still there. I'd never actually heard it before—not like this. Not as a distinct voice separate from my own thinking.

For decades, that loop had been so constant, so ever-present, I'd mistaken it for reality. It wasn't a thought—it was the water I swam in. The air I breathed. The operating system running beneath every decision, every relationship, every moment of my life. It was so fundamental that questioning it would have been like questioning gravity.

Now, with my nervous system finally calm enough to pay attention, I could hear it for what it was:

A lie. Masquerading as truth—*in my voice.*

I sat there in the dim morning light. Stunned. Wondering. How long had this been running? How many decisions had it shaped? How many moments of rest had it stolen? How much of my exhaustion wasn't physical at all—just the cost of outrunning a voice that lived inside my own head?

That morning, I didn't know how to change it. But I could finally see it clearly. After years of unconscious obedience, the loop was exposed—and exposure is the first step to freedom.

The Invisible Narrator

I call them loops.

They're the automatic scripts that run beneath conscious thought. The narratives that feel so fundamental, so obviously true, you never think to question them. They're not just thoughts—they're the lens through which you interpret every thought. The framework through which you filter every experience. The hidden code that shapes every choice before you're even aware you're choosing.

Everyone has them. You have them. Right now, as you're reading this, loops are running in the background of your mind, shaping what you notice. What you believe. And what you think is possible.

Here are the greatest hits—the loops I used to hear most often:

- *I'm only as valuable as what I produce.*

- *If I rest, I'm failing.*

- *People only love the version of me that performs.*

- *I have to hold everything together or it all falls apart.*

- *My needs don't matter as much as everyone else's.*

- *If people really knew me, they'd leave.*

- *I don't deserve good things.*

- *Something bad is always about to happen.*

- *I should be further along by now.*

- *I can't trust anyone completely.*

- *Asking for help is weakness.*

- *I never finish what I start.*

Did any of those land? Did you feel a flicker of recognition—a little jolt of *that's me?*

That's a loop.

And here's what makes them so powerful: they don't announce themselves as beliefs. They present themselves as facts. As simply the way things are. As reality itself. You don't *believe* that you're only valuable when producing—you *know* it, the way you know the sky is blue. It doesn't feel like an interpretation. It feels like truth.

You're not living your life. You're living a story someone else wrote.

And you've been reading from that script so long, you forgot you didn't write it.

Where the Scripts Come From

You weren't born with these scripts. You learned them. Every. Single. One.

Some came from your family. Not necessarily from what was said—sometimes the most powerful loops came from what was never said at all. The praise that only came when you achieved. The love that felt conditional on your behavior. The chaos that taught you to scan for danger. The absence that taught you not to need. The volatility that taught you to be invisible. The perfection that was expected but never modeled.

Children are meaning-making machines. When something painful happens, they don't just experience the pain—they create a story to explain it. And that story, created by a mind too young to understand context or nuance, becomes the operating system they run for decades.

Dad left? *I'm not worth staying for.*

Mom was always stressed? *I'm too much.*

Praise only came for grades? *I only matter when I perform.*

Parents fought all the time? *Love hurts.*

Sibling got all the attention? *I don't exist.*

Kids don't think their way to these conclusions. They swallow them whole—hook, line, and sinker. Before they could question, before they could contextualize, before they could understand that dad left because of his own wounds or mom was stressed because of systems larger than any child could comprehend. The story formed, hardened, and went underground— running silently ever since.

Some loops came from your culture. The messages about what successful people do. The images of who deserves love and who doesn't. The unspoken rules about what's acceptable to feel, to want, to be. The myths about hard work always paying off. The lies about what makes someone valuable.

These cultural loops are particularly insidious because they're reinforced everywhere. Turn on the TV—there's the loop. Scroll social media—there it is again. Listen to the conversation at dinner—same message, different package. When a loop is socially validated, questioning it feels like questioning reality itself.

Some loops came from your experiences. The rejection that became "I'm not enough." The betrayal that became "I can't trust anyone." The failure that became "I don't deserve success." The abandonment that became "Everyone leaves eventually." Those are toxic to your system.

Every significant wound leaves a story in its wake. The wound heals—sort of—but a remnant of the story remains, shaping how you interpret every similar situation that follows. One rejection in tenth grade becomes a lifetime of assuming you'll be rejected. One betrayal by a trusted person becomes a blanket distrust of anyone who gets close.

Some loops came from religion—or what passed for it. Toxic theology teaching you God's love had to be earned. You were born a broken sinner. Shame-based spirituality making you afraid of your own desires. Churches measuring devotion by performance and participation. Sermons telling you your body was the enemy, your doubts were dangerous, your questions were a lack of faith.

I spent my entire life in religious environments. Most of it was life-giving. But some of it installed loops that took years to identify and even longer to uproot.

God is disappointed in you.
You're never doing enough.
Everyone is more important than you.

Your struggles mean your faith is weak.
Faithful people don't have those thoughts.

These spiritual loops are the hardest to confront because they come wrapped in sacred language. Questioning them feels like questioning God—when really, you're just questioning someone's interpretation of God. Someone who may have been just as wounded as you—or worse.

And some loops—maybe the most powerful ones—you invented yourself. Stories you made up to explain pain that didn't make sense. Narratives you constructed as a child to survive situations no child should have to navigate.

These stories were adaptive. At the time, they helped you cope. They helped you make sense of a confusing world. They helped you survive. A child who believes "I'm not worth loving" will stop trying to be loved—which, in an environment where love isn't available, is actually a protective strategy. A child who believes "my needs don't matter" will stop having needs—which, when needs can't be met, reduces constant disappointment.

But survival strategies have a shelf life. And the stories that protected you at seven are probably imprisoning you at forty-seven.

The Loop That Almost Killed Me

Let me tell you where my "productivity equals value" loop came from.

I grew up in a household where worth was measured by contribution. Not explicitly—my parents never sat me down and said, "Tim, you're only valuable when you're useful." They would have been horrified by that statement. They loved me. I know they loved me.

But the message was everywhere. Encoded in what earned attention and what didn't. Written in the invisible ink of a thousand small moments.

Praise came when I achieved. When I brought home the good grades. When I helped without being asked. When I made things easier for everyone else. When I performed well. When I did something noteworthy. On a stage. On a field. Holding a microphone. Saying the right words.

Attention disappeared when I wasn't producing. When I was just being a kid—playing, resting, needing, struggling—I became invisible. Not punished. Just... unseen. The household continued around me like I wasn't quite there. My presence only registered when it was useful. And it got worse as my brothers—six, eight, and ten years older—left the house. One by one they left, and I became even less noticed—even when it was only me.

So I acted out. Got loud. Got in trouble. Pushed buttons until someone had to look at me. Bad attention was still attention. At least when I was a problem, I existed. I didn't have the words for it then, but I was screaming to be seen. And when screaming became normal, I stopped noticing I was doing it.

Eventually the screaming stopped working. So I found other ways to disappear. Substances helped. For a while, anyway. Until they didn't.

A child's brain makes sense of this the only way it can:

I matter when I produce. I disappear when I don't.

That loop got me through adolescence. I did my homework. Fit in everywhere. Worked and went to school. Showed up at church as the perfect preacher's kid. I was the consummate chameleon—because chameleons get noticed.

It made me successful by every external measure.

It also made me incapable of rest. Incapable of receiving love I hadn't earned. Incapable of believing my existence had value beyond my output.

During my health crisis, that loop almost killed me. Because when my body couldn't produce anymore—when the neuralgia made every day a battle just to function—the loop didn't pause. It shifted to condemnation: *You're not producing. So what good are you?*

I didn't consciously believe that. I would have rejected it if anyone had said it out loud. But it was running beneath my conscious thought. And it was pushing me toward a cliff.

If you don't rewrite your story first, pain rewrites it for you. And pain doesn't write kindly.

People Living Someone Else's Script

Picture a surgeon at the top of his field. The guy other surgeons call for the impossible cases. He's built his entire identity on being the best—the one who never fails, never shows weakness, never admits he doesn't know something.

HIS LOOP: *If I'm not the best, I'm nothing.*

He'd probably trace it back to an immigrant father who sacrificed everything to give his children opportunities. The unspoken message: don't waste the sacrifice. Be extraordinary. Anything less is betrayal.

He's been extraordinary. But extraordinary came at a cost. Never taken a real vacation. First marriage ended because he was never home. Relationship with his kids is cordial but distant—he doesn't know how to connect without achievement as the bridge. And at 58, he's starting to notice his hands aren't as steady as they used to be. The end of surgery is approaching, and he has no idea who he is without it.

If you could sit across from someone like this and ask him one question, it might be: "When you can't operate anymore, will you be worthless?"

He probably couldn't answer. The loop wouldn't let him.

Now, picture a mother of four who hasn't made a decision based on her own desires in fifteen years. Every choice runs through a single filter: what do they need?

HER LOOP: *My needs don't matter. Everyone else comes first.*

She'd trace it back to growing up as the oldest of six kids with an overwhelmed single mom. She became the second parent before she hit double digits. Her job was to make things easier, to not add burden, to be the helper. Needing anything for herself felt selfish—almost dangerous.

Now at 45, she's perfected the disappearing act. Her kids are thriving. Her husband is comfortable. And she can't re-member the last time she did something just because she wanted to. She's lost the ability to even know what she wants. The "wanting" part of her has atrophied from disuse.

I'd bet it took a health scare to get her attention—her body's way of demanding what she'd refused to give it. And if you asked her who she is outside of what she does for other people, she wouldn't have an answer. She literally wouldn't know.

Now, picture a VP at a logistics company—the kind of guy from Chapter 1 who can't put his phone down and hasn't slept through the night in years. Behind the phone addiction and the weight gain and the inability to be present is this loop: *If I let my guard down, everything falls apart.*

I'd put money on an unpredictable childhood. Probably an alcoholic parent. The kind of home where you learned to read the room before you learned to read books. Where you scanned constantly—anticipating danger, preparing for the next explosion. Hypervigilance kept you safe when you were seven.

But he isn't seven anymore. He runs a logistics company now. Hypervigilance makes him great at his job—he spots problems before they become crises. But it also means he never, ever relaxes. His nervous system is stuck in permanent scan mode. His body is never off duty. And it's breaking down from the constant alert.

If you asked him why he can't relax, he'd probably say something like, "I don't know how. When I try, I feel more anxious. Like something bad is about to happen if I stop watching for it."

His loop isn't just a thought. It's a physical state his body learned to maintain.

Now, picture a partner at a law firm. Brilliant. Driven. Running on four hours of sleep and pure determination.

HER LOOP: *Rest is weakness.*

This one probably didn't come from childhood. It came from law school. From the culture of relentless competition. From partners who bragged about sleeping at the office, missing their kids' birthdays, working holidays instead of spending them with family. From an industry treating self-destruction as a badge of honor.

Sometimes loops don't come from trauma. Sometimes they come from tribes. From the groups we want to belong to. From the unspoken rules of the systems we've entered. We absorb loops from our professional cultures as powerfully as from our families.

She absorbed her loop to survive in a world rewarding it. But survival is costing her everything else. Her health—chronic migraines, IBS, insomnia. Her marriage—roommates sharing an apartment, nothing more. Her ability to feel anything other than the next deadline.

If you asked her, she'd probably say, "I don't know how to be any other way. This is who I am."

But it's not who she is. It's who she became to survive a system. And survival isn't the same as living.

THE SCIENCE OF LOOPS: LOOP MANAGEMENT

Here's how loops actually work in your brain—and why they're so hard to change.

When you experience something repeatedly, especially with emotional intensity, your brain creates neural pathways to process it efficiently. *What fires together, wires together.* The loop becomes literally encoded in your neural architecture—a well-worn groove that your thoughts naturally flow through.

This is why loops feel like truth. They're not just ideas you have; they're physical structures in your brain. Questioning them feels unnatural because you're trying to fight your own neurology.

But here's the good news: *neuroplasticity is real*. The brain that learned the loop can unlearn it. The neural pathway that was built can be weakened. And a new pathway—a new loop—can be constructed in its place.

This is what I call LOOP MANAGEMENT. It's the systematic process of identifying, interrupting, and replacing the scripts that run your life.

It's not positive thinking. It's not affirmation. It's neurological rewiring through consistent practice.

The process has four steps:

STEP 1: HEAR IT — NAME THE LOOP

You can't change what you can't see. The first step is catching the loop in action—hearing it as a distinct voice rather than experiencing it as reality.

This requires the nervous system regulation from Chapter 1. When your body is in survival mode, you don't have the bandwidth for self-observation. You're too busy surviving to notice the stories driving your survival. But once your nervous system calms, the loops become audible.

The practice: When you feel triggered—anxious, defensive, angry, shut down—pause and ask, "What am I believing right now?" Write it down in this format: "I believe that _______________."

Be specific. Not "I feel bad." But "I believe that if I fail at this project, it proves I'm incompetent and don't deserve my position."

The loop will often sound ridiculous once you write it down. That's good. That's the beginning of its power crumbling.

STEP 2: SOURCE IT — TRACE THE ORIGIN

Once you've named the loop, trace it back. Where did you learn this? Who first spoke this message—explicitly or implicitly? What experience taught you this was true?

This isn't about blame. It's about understanding. When you see where a loop came from, you realize it wasn't inevitable truth—it was learned. And what was learned can be unlearned.

The practice: Ask yourself:

- *When is the earliest I can remember believing this?*

- *Who or what taught me this was true?*

- *What was happening in my life when this loop formed?*

- *How did this belief help me survive at the time?*

The last question is crucial. Most loops were adaptive. They helped you navigate a difficult situation. Honoring that—seeing the loop as a survival strategy rather than a character flaw—creates space for compassion. And compassion makes change possible.

STEP 3: TEST IT — REALITY CHECK

Here's where you put the loop on trial like a defendant in a courtroom. Is it actually true? What's the evidence for and against? What would a neutral observer—a jury of people who actually love you—say?

Most loops fall apart under cross-examination. They're built on a child's logic. Or one bad experience stretched into universal truth. Or someone else's wounds that got pinned on you.

The practice: Ask yourself these questions:

- *Is this actually true, or does it just feel true?*

- *What's the evidence for it? What's the evidence against?*

- *Would I say this to someone I love? (If your daughter failed a project, would you tell her she's incompetent and doesn't deserve her job? No? Then why do you say it to yourself?)*

- *What would someone who loves me say about this belief?*

STEP 4: REPLACE IT — WRITE NEW CODE

You can't just stop believing the old loop. The brain doesn't work that way. You can't delete neural pathways—you have to build new ones that are stronger.

So you need a replacement. Not a bumper sticker. Not something you think you should believe. Something actually true that speaks to the same fear the old loop was trying to protect you from.

The practice: Write a replacement that's:

- *Specific—not "I'm enough" but something to address your actual loop*
- *Believable—something you can accept even if it feels weird at first*
- *Aimed at the same fear—answering the question the old loop was answering*

Here are some examples that have worked for me and others:

Old Loop: I'm only valuable when I produce.

New Code: *My output is not the measure of my worth.*

Old Loop: If I rest, I'm failing.

New Code: *Rest and recovery aren't laziness.*

Old Loop: My needs don't matter.

New Code: *Meeting my needs makes me more available, not less.*

Old Loop: If people really knew me, they'd leave.

New Code: *The people who matter will stay for the real me.*

Old Loop: Something bad is about to happen.

New Code: *I've survived so far, so I can handle whatever comes.*

Here's the truth beneath all of it: You've been telling yourself someone else's story. A story written by wounds you didn't choose, systems you didn't design, and fears you inherited before you knew any better.

It's time to write your own.

Tell yourself a different story with a better ending. Say it until you believe it. Then live it until it becomes true.

That's not denial. It's not positive thinking. It's neurological rewiring—choosing the narrative that serves your becoming instead of the one that kept you small.

Why Your Body Fights Your Mind

Here's the part nobody talks about—and it's the reason so many people stay stuck even after they've done the inner work.

Your body is addicted to your emotions.

I don't mean that metaphorically. I mean it the way I'd mean it about alcohol or nicotine or any other chemical dependency. Your cells have literally become addicted to the chemistry of whatever emotional state you've lived in longest.

Let me explain how this works, because understanding it changed everything for me.

Every time you feel an emotion—anger, anxiety, shame, fear—your brain releases specific chemicals into your bloodstream. These chemicals travel to every cell in your body. And here's the thing: your cells have receptors for those chemicals. They receive them like a key fitting into a lock.

When you feel anxious for years—like I did—your cells build more receptors for anxiety. When you feel shame repeatedly, your cells start craving that chemistry. When stress becomes your baseline, your body adapts to expect it.

Your cells don't care if an emotion is destroying your life. They just want what's familiar. They want their fix.

This is why you can know something intellectually and still keep falling back into the same patterns. Your conscious mind might be ready to change. But your body? Your body is living in the past. And most of the time, it's running the show.

I experienced this during my recovery in ways I couldn't explain at first. There were days when I'd start to feel genuinely hopeful—really hopeful, for the first time in months—and within hours, my mind would manufacture reasons to return to despair. Not because hope was naive. Because despair was familiar. My cells knew that chemistry. They were comfortable there.

The anxiety I'd carried for decades wasn't just a mental habit. It was a physiological addiction. My body didn't want peace. It wanted what it knew.

Think about what this means.

By the time you're an adult, roughly 95% of who you are isn't running from your conscious mind at all. It's running from your subconscious—which is really just another word for your body. Your memorized emotional patterns. Your habitual reactions. The chemical states your cells have learned to expect and demand.

You wake up in the morning, and before you've had a single conscious thought, your body has already flooded you with the familiar chemicals of yesterday's emotions. You haven't even gotten out of bed, and you're already feeling anxious or stressed or defeated. Not because of anything happening now. Because your body is recreating the past.

This is why willpower fails.

You're not fighting a bad habit. You're fighting a chemical dependency at the cellular level.

Every time you try to think a new thought, feel a new feeling, or become a new person—your body throws a tantrum. It sends signals to your brain that something's wrong. It creates discomfort, restlessness, even physical symptoms. And your brain, trying to restore balance, generates thoughts that justify returning to the familiar emotional state.

"This isn't working." "Who are you kidding?" "You'll never really change."

Those aren't insights. They're not your intuition warning you.
Those are withdrawal symptoms. Your body fighting to get its fix.

This changes everything about how we approach transformation.

You can't just think your way to a new life. You can't affirm your way out of cellular addiction. You can't positive-think past a nervous system that's been marinating in stress hormones for years.

This is why the regulation work in Chapter 1 isn't optional. It's foundational.

You have to change the chemical environment of your body before new thoughts can take root. You have to teach your cells that a new emotional baseline is safe. You have to experience peace, calm, and safety long enough that your body stops treating them as threats.

The body must believe before the mind can change. And your body only believes what it experiences repeatedly.

So when you're doing the LOOP MANAGEMENT work—naming the loop, sourcing it, testing it, replacing it—understand that you're not just changing your thinking. You're breaking an addiction. And like any addiction, the withdrawal is real. The resistance is real. The pull back toward the familiar is real.

But here's what I've learned: the body that learned to crave stress can learn to crave peace. The cells that built receptors for anxiety can build receptors for calm. The nervous system that memorized chaos can memorize coherence.

It just takes longer than we want. And it requires patience with a body that's doing its best to keep you alive using the only methods it knows.

WHAT CHANGES: BEFORE AND AFTER

Before you heal your story, you live in reaction.

The loop runs, you respond, and you don't even realize you had a choice. Life feels like it's happening to you rather than through you. Every trigger pulls the same response. Every situation confirms the same story. And every day reinforces the same beliefs.

You feel like a puppet whose strings you can't see. You keep ending up in the same patterns—same types of relationships, same conflicts at work, same feelings of inadequacy despite external indications. You know something's wrong but can't put your finger on it. The problem seems to be everywhere and nowhere at the same time.

Your emotional life feels out of control. Small things trigger big responses. You overreact, then feel ashamed of overreacting, then stuff the feelings down until they explode again.

Rinse. Lather. Repeat.

And beneath it all, there's an exhaustion that sleep doesn't begin to touch. Because you're not just tired from doing—you're tired from being at war with yourself. Tired from fighting a voice that lives in your own head.

After the rewrite, something shifts.

There's space now. Between what happens and how you respond. A moment where you get to choose.

The trigger still comes. The loop still fires. But you catch it. You see it before it takes over. And you've got a different story ready—one you wrote, one that's true, one that fits who you're becoming.

I remember the first time I felt this shift. I was in a meeting where a direction I was suggesting was being dismissed. Some of the criticism was fair; some wasn't. Old me would have gone into defense mode immediately—justifying, explaining, protecting my value through my output. Fighting for my right to be seen as valuable.

But I felt the loop start. Felt the familiar grip of "your value is on the line." Felt the adrenaline surge that always preceded my defensive response.

And instead of reacting, I paused. Took a breath. Reminded myself: "My value exists before my output."

Then I responded differently. I listened to the criticism. Acknowledged what was valid. Offered to improve what could be improved. And I didn't feel like I was dying inside while I did it.

That was when I knew the rewrite was working. Not because the loop was gone—it wasn't. But because it no longer had the power to control me.

That surgeon from earlier? Imagine he spends sixty years believing he's only as good as his surgical skill. You don't undo that overnight. But he could start noticing the loop before it takes over. He could begin asking a question that would've seemed absurd before: "What if I matter even when I'm not operating?"

New Code: *My value isn't in my hands.*

He'd still do surgery. But maybe he'd start mentoring residents. Reconnecting with his kids. Building furniture in his garage on weekends. The loop would still fire. He just wouldn't believe it anymore.

That mother who forgot herself? She could start asking one question: "What do I want right now?" Fifteen years of disappearing had almost killed that part of her. At first, she'd have no answer.

New Code: *My wants matter too.*

She'd keep asking. Coffee on the porch—alone. A novel. A pottery class she'd put off for a decade. Small things. But each one would say she existed outside of what she did for everyone else.

Her daughter might tell her, "Mom, you seem different. Like you're actually here now."

That hypervigilant VP? He'd have to learn he isn't eight anymore. His dad was a drunk. Scanning for danger kept him alive back then. Problem is, his nervous system never got the memo that he left that house forty years ago.

New Code: *I can pay attention without being afraid.*

He'd still be sharp. Still spot problems early. But there's a difference between alert and terrified. And he'd be learning it—slowly.

That law partner? She'd have it hardest—her whole world reinforces the lie. Law school. Partners. Billable hours. Rest is weakness.

So she'd test it. The partners she admired—long careers, still married, kids who called them back—weren't the all-nighter heroes. They'd figured out something else.

New Code: *Rest is how I stay in this game.*

Her hours might dip. But results would go up. Migraines would stop. And her marriage would recover. She'd make partner anyway.

THE SPIRITUAL DIMENSION

There's another layer here we can't skip. One that goes beyond psychology and neuroscience.

The enemy of your soul doesn't need to destroy you. He just needs to keep you believing a lie.

If you can be convinced you're worthless, you'll never step into your purpose. If you can be convinced you're alone, you'll never risk connection. If you can be convinced change is impossible, you'll never try. If you can be convinced rest is weakness, you'll destroy yourself before you ever become who you were meant to be.

The loops aren't just psychological patterns. They're spiritual strongholds—lies that have been reinforced so many times they feel like identity. They're the whispers of an enemy who knows destroyed potential is as effective as destroyed life, and far easier to accomplish.

But here's the truth that can set you free—the loops are not your identity. They're imposters. Stealing your voice. Using your memories. Masquerading as you.

The truth about who you are was spoken before any wound was inflicted. Before any rejection shaped you. Before any failure defined you. Before any system told you who to be.

You were made in the image of the Divine. You were called beloved before you ever performed. You were enough before you achieved anything—and you'll be enough long after your achievements are forgotten. Don't let anyone tell you differently—that faith is fear-based.

The loops tell you that your worth is conditional. That you have to earn love. That you're one mistake away from being abandoned. That you're only as good as your last performance.

The truth says otherwise.

This is why LOOP MANAGEMENT isn't merely a psychological technique. When you name the loop, you're calling out the lie. When you source it, you're understanding how it got in. When you test it, you're holding it up against actual truth. When you replace it, you're speaking what's real over what's false.

It's not just therapy. It's not just positive thinking.

It's something closer to exorcism—evicting the lies that have taken up residence in your mind and replacing them with what was always true.

THE DAILY PRACTICE

Identifying your loops isn't a one-time event. It's an ongoing practice.

I still catch old loops running—sometimes the same ones I thought I'd rewritten. Neural pathways don't die; they just get weaker when they're not reinforced. Stress, fatigue, or triggering circumstances can reactivate loops that have been dormant for years. You'll think you've beaten one, and then a crisis hits, and there it is again, playing like it never left.

The goal isn't to eliminate all loops. The goal is to build awareness—to catch the loop before it runs the show. To have a gap between the loop's appearance and your response. To be able to say "I see you" rather than "I am you."

Here's my daily practice:

MORNING LOOP CHECK (3 MINUTES): Before I check anything or talk to anyone, I take three minutes to notice what's running in my head. What am I already believing about this day? What story am I already telling about what's going to happen? If there's a loop playing—and there usually is—I name it. Write it down. Then I consciously choose a different story. How do I control it? I start by reciting my mission, priorities, and goals. In other words, I choose my narrative first.

EVENING LOOP REVIEW (5 MINUTES): I review the day with one question: Where did my intentions get hijacked? Where did I react from old programming instead of responding from present awareness? No shame. No judgment. Just observation. Then I trace the reaction back to the loop that drove it. I can usually find the moment I let it win.

WEEKLY LOOP AUDIT (15 MINUTES): Once a week, usually Sunday evening, I look at my journal and ask: What patterns am I seeing? Which loops are showing up most often? What situations trigger them? Am I making progress, or am I stuck? If I'm honest in my journal, it's a reliable narrator.

This practice takes maybe ten minutes daily, plus a weekly review. It's not elaborate. But over time, it builds a kind of inner awareness—a spectator seat where you can watch your thoughts without being consumed by them.

The loops don't disappear. But they lose their power. They become something you have rather than something you are.

The Resistance You'll Face

The loop will fight to survive. When you start naming and testing loops, expect backlash. The loop has been running the show for decades. It doesn't want to be dethroned. It will get louder. It will find new evidence. It will recruit other loops to support it.

This is normal. It's actually a sign that you're making progress. The loop wouldn't fight this hard if it weren't threatened.

The people who benefit from your loops won't celebrate your change. Some relationships are built on your dysfunction. The friend who needs you to be the caretaker. The boss who needs you to be the over-worker. The family member who needs you to be the responsible one who never has needs. When you start rewriting loops, these dynamics shift—and not everyone will be happy about it.

This is also normal. And it reveals which relationships are based on mutual growth versus mutual dysfunction.

Old loops can be triggered by stress. You'll think you've rewritten a loop, and then a crisis hits, and boom—there it is again, playing like you never touched it. This isn't failure. It's how the brain works. Under stress, we default to older patterns. The practice is returning to the new loop after the stress passes, not expecting perfection during the storm.

The Mantra

You're not broken. You're running code you didn't write.

Say it until you believe it. Say it on the days when the old loops are screaming and the new story feels like a lie.

Every loop was learned. Every script was absorbed. Every lie was installed by something or someone outside you.

Which means every loop can be unlearned. Every script can be rewritten. Every lie can be replaced with truth.

You're not stuck with this programming forever. You can write your own code.

Reflection Questions

1. What loop runs loudest in your head? What's the most destructive thought that plays on repeat?

2. Where did you learn it? Can you trace it back to a family pattern, a cultural message, a specific wound, a survival strategy?

3. What would your life look like if you didn't believe it anymore? What decisions would you make differently? What risks would you take? What would you stop tolerating?

THE INVITATION

Your body is learning to feel safe. Now your mind is learning to tell the truth.

This is where transformation starts to compound. A regulated body plus a rewritten story equals a person who can actually change—not just for a moment, but for a lifetime.

The next chapter takes you deeper: into the integration of body, mind, and spirit that makes lasting change possible. But that integration requires the foundation you're building now.

Keep naming the loops. Keep testing them against truth. Keep writing new code.

Your story is being rewritten. And you're finally the one holding the pen.

Continue this practice. Scan for the free daily companion app.

— **I** —

Integrate the Whole

Stop fragmenting yourself to fit broken systems.

I was sitting in my office. Shuffling notes. Staring at a tele-prompter. Trying to film a course about balance while my body was anything but balanced.

The course is called WHOLECARE™—six stages for leaders to find equilibrium in their lives. Ironic, right? I was teaching integration while feeling completely fragmented.

I'd spent over thirty years feeding off the energy of live audiences. Reading the room. Adjusting on the fly. Feeling the collective breath of a crowd and riding it like a wave. That was my gift—connection in real time, presence that couldn't be faked.

But this was my new normal. A camera lens instead of faces. A teleprompter instead of intuition. Notes on a computer screen I had to glance at without looking like I was glancing. All of it needing to feel authentic and natural when nothing about it felt authentic or natural.

My producer was there, trying to direct the project, doing his best to help me get through it. But his presence only added to the pressure. Another person watching me fail. Another witness to the gap between the guy who used to own a stage and the guy who couldn't get through a two-minute segment without stumbling.

This setup was supposed to save me. Keep me off planes. Let me get my life back while I managed my health and found a way forward. But in that moment, it felt like a prison.

My chest was tight. My thoughts were scattered. I'd recorded the same segment four times and still couldn't land it. The words on the teleprompter—words I'd written, words I believed—felt foreign in my mouth. Like I was reading someone else's script about someone else's life.

I tried pushing through. Told myself to focus. Reminded myself I'd done harder things than this. Recited the mental pep talk I'd given to thousands of other people in similar moments.

Nothing worked.

Finally, I stopped. Not strategically—I just couldn't do it anymore. I told my producer I needed a minute, pushed back from the desk, walked outside, and stood there. No plan. No technique. Just the need to not be in that room for another second.

The air was cool. I hadn't noticed how shallow my breathing had become until I took a real breath—the kind that fills your lungs instead of just moving your shoulders. I felt my feet on the ground. Heard traffic I'd been too locked in to notice. Let my shoulders drop from wherever they'd been hiding near my ears.

And then something shifted.

Not dramatically. Not instantly. But gradually, like fog lifting. The thoughts that had been jammed started to loosen. The tightness in my chest released. And somewhere in the space that opened up, I remembered why I was making this course in the first place. Not for the camera. For the people who would eventually watch it. People who were stuck like I'd been stuck. People who needed what I'd learned.

I went back inside. Filmed the segment in one take. I hadn't changed my thinking. I'd changed my state—and my thinking followed.

That was when I finally understood something I'd been circling for months: I'd spent my *whole life* treating body, mind, and spirit like separate departments. Separate problems requiring separate solutions. Physical health over here, managed by doctors and diet. Mental health over there, addressed by therapy and self-help books. Spiritual health in another room entirely, the domain of church and prayer.

But they weren't separate. They never had been. They were one system—intricately connected, constantly communicating, designed to work together.

And when they work together, everything changes.

The Science of Wholeness

I'd heard the word coherence before. In vague contexts—people talking about living a coherent life, getting your story straight, having your act together. But this was different. This was physiological. Measurable. Objective.

Coherence isn't a feeling. It isn't a metaphor. It's a state your body can actually achieve—a state where your heart, brain, and nervous system stop fighting each other and start working together.

Research from the HeartMath Institute has spent decades studying heart-brain communication. Most people don't know this, but your heart sends more signals to your brain than your brain sends to your heart. It's not just a pump—it's an information processing center. It has its own neural network, sometimes called the heart brain. And the signals it sends profoundly affect your emotional state, your cognitive function, even your perception of reality.

When your heart rhythm is chaotic—which it is during stress, anxiety, frustration—it sends chaotic signals to your brain. Your brain interprets those signals as evidence that something is wrong. It stays on high alert. It suppresses higher cognitive function. It keeps you in survival mode.

But when your heart rhythm is coherent—smooth, rhythmic, ordered—it sends a completely different message. All is well. You're safe. You can think clearly now.

Coherence isn't just about feeling better. It physically changes what's possible. In a coherent state, your prefrontal cortex comes fully online. You have access to creativity, problem-solving, emotional regulation. The parts of you that were offline during stress become available again.

This isn't meditation mysticism. It's measurement. Science. Proof that your body, mind, and spirit can actually work together. Can actually align.

And it can happen through something as simple as intentional breathing.

THE LIE OF FRAGMENTATION

We've been taught to split ourselves.

Mind from body. Logic from emotion. Work from life. Sacred from secular. Strength from tenderness. Success from rest. Public self from private self. The person we are from the person we show.

We learn these divisions early. School teaches us that thinking happens in our heads, separate from what our bodies feel. We sit in chairs for hours, ignoring physical signals, training ourselves to treat the body as an inconvenience that carries the mind around.

Work teaches us to leave our personal selves at the door. "Don't bring your problems to the office." "Check your emotions at the door." "Be professional"—which usually means be less human.

Religion often teaches us that the body is suspect—something to control, overcome, mortify, or ignore. That physical pleasure is dangerous. That emotional experience is untrustworthy. That true spirituality transcends the messy reality of being embodied creatures.

And so we fragment. We become experts at compartmentalization. We develop different selves for different contexts—work self, home self, church self, online self—and barely notice when they contradict each other.

We learn to suppress certain emotions because they're not "appropriate." We ignore physical signals because we have deadlines to meet. We push spiritual questions to Sunday because Monday through Friday doesn't have time for mystery.

This fragmentation isn't wisdom. It isn't maturity. It isn't what healthy adults do.

It's survival.

We learned to split ourselves because the systems we were born into couldn't handle all of us.

Our families needed us in certain roles. Our schools needed us to sit still and comply. Our workplaces need the productive parts, not the whole human. Our cultures reward the performance, not the person.

The whole human was too much. Too complex. Too inconvenient. Too unpredictable.

So we adapted. We became fragments of ourselves, presenting whatever piece the moment required. We got good at the costume changes, the quick switches, the seamless transitions between versions.

And we called it growing up.

You weren't made in parts. Stop living like you were.

The Cost of Division

Fragmentation has a price. And most of us have been pay-ing it for so long we don't even notice anymore. We've absorbed the cost as normal—as just how life feels.

When you separate your body from your decisions, you make choices that slowly destroy your health. You push through pain signals designed to protect you. You ignore fatigue that's warning you of burnout. You treat your physical self like a ma-chine to be optimized rather than a partner to be honored. And then you're surprised when the machine breaks down.

When you separate your emotions from your logic, you make "rational" decisions that leave you empty. You build a life that looks right on paper but feels hollow in your heart. You achieve goals that don't satisfy because you chose them with only half of yourself. You optimize for optics while ignoring meaning.

When you separate your spirit from your daily life, you ex-perience a nagging sense that something's missing—even when you have everything you thought you wanted. You accumulate success but not significance. You fill your calendar but not your soul. The transcendent gets pushed to weekends and holidays, and you're left with a life that's efficient but meaningless.

When you maintain different selves for different contexts, you exhaust yourself with the performance. The mental ener-gy required to track which version you're supposed to be right now. The anxiety of being "found out"—of someone from one context meeting the you from another context. The deep loneliness of never being fully known because you've never been fully present.

I lived this division for decades.

I was a pastor—a professional spiritual person—but my spirit was compartmentalized to sermon prep and marriage counseling and the occasional retreat. The rest of my life was run by productivity loops and survival instincts that had nothing to do with anything sacred.

My body was a tool for ministry, not a partner in it. Something to be caffeinated, disciplined, and pushed through obstacles. I was proud of how little sleep I could function on, how many hours I could work without eating, how I could ignore physical limits in service of my "calling" to the Lord.

My emotions were things to manage, not messages to heed. Sadness was weakness. Anger was sin. Fear was a lack of faith. So I tamped them down, pushed them aside, performed composure while chaos churned underneath.

And I showed different versions to different audiences. The confident leader at work. The exhausted husband and father at home. The polished preacher on stage. The anxious wreck at 3am when no one was watching.

Is it any wonder my body broke down?

I wasn't living as a whole person. I was a committee of competing parts. Each one pulling in its own direction. None of them talking to the others. All of them exhausting themselves in the effort of maintaining the illusion they were somehow one person.

Integration isn't a luxury. It isn't something you get to after you've handled the urgent stuff. It's the foundation. Without it, everything you build will eventually crack—because it's built on division.

THE STACK

I think of integration in terms of what I call THE STACK: body, mind, spirit—layered on top of each other, connected, interdependent.

Not body or mind or spirit. Not body versus mind versus spirit. But body *with* mind *with* spirit. All three, working together, informing each other, supporting each other.

The body is the foundation. We covered this in Chapter 1. If your body isn't regulated—if your nervous system is stuck in survival mode—nothing else works right. You can't think clearly when cortisol is flooding your brain. You can't hear your emotions when your threat-detection system is running at full volume. You can't access spiritual depth when your entire being is focused on survival.

The body has to stabilize first. Not because it's more important than mind or spirit, but because it's the foundation the others rest on. You can't build the second floor until the first floor exists.

The mind builds on the body. Once you're regulated, you can actually hear your thoughts. You can identify your loops—like we did in Chapter 2. You can choose different stories, test old beliefs, replace inherited scripts with new ones.

Mental work becomes possible when the body provides a stable platform. The insights that bounce off a dysregulated nervous system can actually land. The truth you've been trying to believe becomes believable—not because it's more true, but because you're finally able to receive it.

The spirit rises from both. When your body is calm and your mind is clear, spiritual awareness opens naturally. You don't have to force it. You don't have to manufacture it. It emerges—like sunlight through a window that's finally been cleaned.

This is why so many spiritual practices feel empty when you try them in a dysregulated state. Prayer becomes another item on the to-do list. Meditation becomes an exercise in frustration. Scripture feels like dead words because there's no bandwidth to let them come alive.

But stack them right—regulate the body, clear the mind—and the spirit is right there. It was always there. You just couldn't access it.

This is why I don't separate the scientific from the spiritual. They're not competing frameworks. They're not opposing worldviews you have to choose between. They're complementary languages for the same reality—like describing an elephant in English and French. Different words, same beast.

The research on heart rate variability isn't contradicting prayer; it's explaining why prayer works. The neuroscience of neural pathways isn't dismissing spiritual formation; it's measuring its effects. The biology of stress response isn't competing with faith; it's showing how faith changes biology.

THE STACK isn't about choosing one approach over another. It's about using all of them together—in the right order, with appropriate attention to each layer.

THE SCIENCE OF INTEGRATION

Modern research has given us remarkable insight into how integration actually works in the body.

The HeartMath Institute has spent over thirty years studying heart-brain communication. Their research shows that the heart's electromagnetic field is sixty times greater in amplitude than the brain's. It can be measured several feet outside the body. And it changes based on emotional state—negative emotions produce chaotic patterns, positive emotions produce coherent ones.

More remarkably, their studies show that heart coherence affects not just the individual experiencing it, but people nearby. Your coherent heart rhythm can actually influence the nervous systems of people around you—a phenomenon called social coherence. This is why we feel calmer around certain people and more anxious around others. We're literally responding to the coherence or chaos of their heart fields.

Neuroscience has mapped the gut-brain axis—the bidirectional communication pathway between your gastrointestinal system and your brain. Your gut contains about 500 million neurons, sometimes called the "second brain." It produces 95% of your body's serotonin—a neurotransmitter critical for mood regulation. When your gut is inflamed or imbalanced, your brain gets the message. When your brain is stressed, your gut feels it.

This is why anxiety often shows up as digestive issues. Why stress affects appetite. Why what you eat influences how you think. The body and mind aren't separate systems occasionally influencing each other—they're one integrated system, constantly communicating through chemical and electrical signals.

Research on interoception—your ability to sense internal body states—shows that people with higher interoceptive awareness have better emotional regulation, clearer decision-making, and stronger mental health. Being able to feel what's happening in your body isn't just nice to have—it's essential for psychological wellbeing.

The science is clear: we are integrated beings. Body affects mind. Mind affects body. Both affect spirit. Spirit affects both. The divisions we've been taught are artificial—cultural constructs that don't match biological reality.

Which means the path to health isn't treating each system separately. *It's learning how to help them work together.*

The Practices of Integration

So how do you actually integrate? How do you move from fragmented parts to functioning whole?

It starts with listening.

Most of us have stopped listening to ourselves. We've learned to override our body's signals, dismiss our emotions, and defer our spiritual questions. Integration begins when you start paying attention again—not to what you think you should be experiencing, but to what you actually are.

PRACTICE 1: BODY CHECK-INS

Throughout the day, pause and ask:

What is my body telling me right now?

Not what you think it should be telling you. Not what's convenient to feel. What's actually there.

Is there tension? Where? Is there energy or fatigue? What does your gut feel like—settled or churning? What about your jaw—clenched or relaxed? Your shoulders—hunched or relaxed? Your breath—shallow or full?

These aren't random sensations. They're information. Your body is constantly communicating about what it needs, what it's afraid of, what it's processing. But if you've spent decades ignoring it, you've probably stopped hearing.

I have a mindfulness app on my Apple watch. When it goes off, I stop whatever I'm doing and scan my body. Just sixty seconds. What am I feeling physically? No judgment. No fixing. Just noticing.

This simple practice has caught tension I wasn't aware of, fatigue I was pushing through, and signals that something needed attention long before it became a crisis. My body knew things my mind was trying to ignore.

PRACTICE 2: COHERENT BREATHING

Six seconds in, six seconds out. That's it. No special posture required. No mantras. No equipment. Just breath at a specific rhythm.

Here's why it works: at approximately five breaths per minute—which is the six-in, six-out rhythm—your heart rate naturally synchronizes with your breath. Your heart rate variability shifts from chaotic to rhythmic. And your nervous system receives a clear, sustained signal: *safe, safe, safe.*

The HeartMath Institute's research shows that coherent heart rhythms send different signals to the brain than chaotic ones. Coherent rhythms activate the prefrontal cortex, enhance emotional regulation, and improve cognitive function. Chaotic rhythms do the opposite—they keep higher brain functions suppressed and survival circuits activated.

In other words: how you breathe literally changes how you think and feel. Not metaphorically. Physiologically.

I practice coherent breathing twice a day—morning and evening, three to five minutes each time. Once again, my watch sends me reminders. But I also use it situationally. Before a difficult conversation. After receiving bad news. When I feel the old loops starting to play. When I notice my body tensing in anticipation of threat.

Six seconds in. Six seconds out. And within a minute, I can feel the shift. The grip loosens. The chaos calms. The parts of me that were pulling in different directions start to align.

This isn't mystical. It's mechanical. It's your body's built-in reset button—one that most people never learn to use.

PRACTICE 3: THE INTEGRATION QUESTION

There's one question I ask myself every day. It's become my north star for integration:

What does my body know that my mind is ignoring?

The first time I asked it, I was surprised by the answer.

My mind was telling me to push through, finish the project, keep going. I had deadlines. People were counting on me. Stopping wasn't an option.

But when I paused and asked what my body knew, the answer was immediate and clear: *You need to stop. Now. Before something breaks.*

My body knew I was heading toward another collapse. My mind was too invested in the outcome, too attached to the identity of being productive to notice the warning signs.

I've learned to trust this question. Not because my body is always right—sometimes fear speaks through physical sensation too. But because it holds information my mind habitually dismisses.

The tension in my shoulders during a meeting might mean something. The knot in my stomach before a commitment might be wisdom, not weakness. The fatigue that won't lift might be more than tiredness—it might be my body refusing to participate in something my soul has already rejected.

Integration isn't about letting your body override your mind. It's about letting them inform each other. It's about making decisions with all of you, not just the part that thinks it's in charge.

PRACTICE 4: THE DAILY STACK REVIEW

Most evenings—not all—I'm not a machine, I do what I call a STACK REVIEW. Five minutes, three questions:

Body: How did I honor my body today? Did I give it rest when it needed rest? Movement when it needed movement? Fuel that nourished rather than depleted? Where did I override its signals, and why?

Mind: How did I care for my mind today? Did I feed it truth or let the loops run unchecked? Did I create space for thinking, or was I reactive all day? What thoughts need attention tomorrow?

Spirit: How did I tend my spirit today? Did I make any room for stillness, wonder, connection to something beyond myself? Did I live from my core values or just from my schedule? Where did I feel most alive, and where most hollow?

I'm not looking for perfection. Most days, I score mediocre on at least one layer of the stack. The point isn't to judge—it's to notice. To see patterns. To catch drift before it becomes disaster.

Over time, this review has become one of my most valuable practices. It keeps me honest about where I am. It keeps me integrated when life tries to fragment me. It keeps me from living as parts when I was made to live as a whole.

PEOPLE LEARNING TO BE WHOLE

Picture a software engineer in Seattle. Brilliant coder. Twenty years of solving complex problems through pure cognition.

If you asked him what his body was feeling, he'd look at you like you'd asked him to explain the meaning of life.

"I don't... feel my body," he'd probably say. "I just use it to carry my brain around."

That's not unusual for people who've spent years living from the neck up. They literally lose connection to physical sensation. They can debug code for twelve hours without noticing hunger. Push through pain until injury forces them to stop. The body becomes an afterthought—infrastructure for the only part of themselves they value.

The path back starts simple. Every morning, before opening the laptop, one question: *Body, what do you need?*

The first few days, nothing. Silence. It's like trying to tune into a radio station that's been turned off for years.

But you keep asking. Every morning. The same question. Listening for any response.

By week two, faint signals start to emerge. *Water. I'm thirsty.* Simple. Basic. Almost embarrassingly obvious. But it's a start.

Then: *My back hurts. I've been sitting wrong.* Then: *I'm tired. Actually tired, not just bored.*

Six months later, everything's different. Taking breaks when the body asks for them—before the pain forces it. Stopping work when tension builds—before the headaches arrive. Still brilliant. Maybe more so, because there's no burnout every three months.

"I didn't realize how much bandwidth I was losing to ignored signals," someone like this might say. "All that energy spent overriding my body—it's available now. For actual work. For actual life."

Now, picture a woman raised in a faith tradition that distrusted emotion. Feelings were suspect—dangerous, deceptive, not to be trusted. "The heart is deceitful above all things," her grandmother would quote. So she learned to compose herself. To maintain control. To never let them see her sweat.

By forty-five, she's a master of composure and a stranger to herself.

Her marriage is dying. Her husband says he feels like he's married to a robot. She doesn't disagree. "I know I'm supposed to feel things," she might say. "I just... don't know how. Or maybe I forgot."

Integration for someone like this means learning to feel again. Not performing emotion—actually experiencing it. Letting herself be moved without immediately controlling the movement.

It starts with naming. When she notices a physical sensation—tightness, warmth, trembling, heaviness—she tries to name the emotion connected to it. Often she can't. The vocabulary isn't there. Forty-five years of suppression has atrophied the muscle.

So it builds slowly, word by word. *That tightness in your chest—could that be anxiety? That heat in your face—might that be anger? That ache behind your eyes—is that possibly sadness?*

It takes a year. There's no shortcut for decades of disconnection. But she learns to feel without falling apart. To let emotions move through her without being controlled by them. To be present to her own inner life without drowning in it.

Her husband notices first: "I finally feel like I'm married to a person."

She cries when he says it. Actually cries. Tears streaming down her face while she sits there, not trying to stop them. Not apologizing. Just letting them be.

"That's the first time in forty years I've cried without trying to make it stop," she might say. "I didn't know I could."

Now, picture a pastor in a traditional church. Twenty years of ministry. He preaches vulnerability from the pulpit while practicing invincibility in private. He has answers for everyone else's spiritual questions while ignoring his own.

"I'm supposed to be the one who has it together," he'd say. "How can I lead people to God if I'm struggling to find Him myself? How can I preach peace when I'm falling apart inside?" (I could be this guy.)

This is fragmentation with a spiritual twist—the lie that leaders must be whole before they can help others. That doubt disqualifies. That questions undermine authority. That you can only serve from your strength, never from your wounds.

Integration for someone like this means bringing private struggles into the public role. Not oversharing. Not making every sermon about personal issues. But letting the congregation see that he's a fellow traveler, not a finished product. That faith and doubt can coexist as dance partners. That questions are as sacred as answers.

He starts small. Mentions his own doubts when preaching on faith. Acknowledges his fatigue when encouraging rest. Lets them see the questions beneath his answers. Lets them catch glimpses of the whole person behind the pastoral role.

"I thought they'd lose respect for me," he might say. "I thought they'd stop coming, stop trusting, stop believing. Instead, they started coming to me with things they'd never shared before. Because they finally believed I'd understand."

His church doesn't shrink. It grows. Not because he has more answers. But because he stops pretending to have them all.

Now, picture a nurse in an urban emergency department. Twelve years of trauma, crisis, and death. She's built walls so high she can't feel anything—at work or at home.

"You have to compartmentalize," she'd say. "If I felt everything I saw, I'd never make it through a shift. So I learned to turn it off."

The problem is, she can't turn it back on. The walls she built for work have become walls for life. She's numb to her children. Distant from her husband. Going through the motions of a life that looks fine from the outside but feels empty from within.

Integration for someone like this is tricky—because complete openness isn't the goal. She needs those walls at work. The question is whether she can make them doors—walls that can open when it's safe and close when it's not.

A transition ritual helps. Fifteen minutes between leaving the hospital and arriving home. Coherent breathing in the car. Asking her body what it's holding from the shift. Consciously setting down the professional armor before walking through her front door.

It takes months. The walls don't want to become doors—they've been walls for too long. But gradually, she finds her way back. Finds she can hold the pain of work without letting it flood her home. Finds she can feel joy with her children without it making work unbearable.

"I'm the same person at work and at home now," she might say. "I just access different parts of myself in different places. But they're connected. They know about each other. I'm not two people anymore—I'm one person in different contexts."

That's integration. Not eliminating appropriate boundaries—creating doors where there used to be walls.

THE SPIRITUAL DIMENSION

You weren't made fragmented. Culture conditioned you.

Go back to nearly any ancient wisdom tradition and you'll find the same understanding: humans are integrated beings. Body, mind, and spirit woven together—not as separate compartments but as one unified system.

The Hebrew creation poem describes it beautifully. Humans formed from dust—earth, ground, physical matter. Then breath enters. The *ruach*—spirit, wind, the animating force of life itself. The sacred and the physical weren't separate. They were joined in the same moment, the same act, the same being.

Every tradition that fragments the human—body bad, spirit good; flesh dangerous, soul pure; emotions deceptive, logic trustworthy—is a departure from that original design. It's philosophy dressed up as wisdom. It's not spiritual maturity. It's cultural distortion.

The great healers and teachers throughout history understood this. They didn't just address the mind or the spirit in isolation. They touched bodies. They honored emotion. They wept. They ate with people. They understood that the sacred doesn't float above the physical—it moves through it.

If the Divine thought matter was beneath it, it wouldn't have created it with such care.

When you integrate—when you honor your body as sacred, your emotions as messengers, your mind as gift—you're not becoming something new. You're returning to something original. You're remembering what was true before culture taught you to forget.

The same creative force that spoke galaxies into existence also formed you. Body, mind, and spirit as one system. Not three parts occasionally interacting—one whole, designed to work in concert.

Every intentional breath can be a prayer. Every grounding movement can be worship. Every coherent heartbeat can be an act of faith.

What Changes

Before integration, you toggle between versions of yourself. Work you. Home you. Public you. Private you. Each context gets a different character, and you barely notice the switches anymore. You've gotten so good at the costume changes that you've forgotten you're wearing costumes.

After integration, you show up the same everywhere. Not rigidly—you still adapt to contexts, still have appropriate boundaries, still bring different energies to different situations. But there's a core that doesn't change depending on the room. People experience the same person across situations.

And so do you.

I noticed this shift about six weeks after implementing my first integration practices. I was in a meeting that would have triggered performance mode in the old days—important people, high stakes, lots of room for impression management. The old me would have armored up, performed competence, calculated every word.

But I found myself remaining centered. Speaking honestly. Not calculating what they wanted to hear, just saying what was true. Acknowledging uncertainty when I didn't know. Admitting mistakes when I'd been wrong.

Afterward, a colleague said, "You seem different lately. More... real. I don't know how else to describe it." It was a huge validation to me.

He couldn't name what had changed. But he could feel it. The fragments were coming together. The performance was ending. The whole person was starting to show up.

There's a peace that comes with integration. Not the absence of problems—those don't go away. Not the absence of stress—life still brings challenges. But the absence of internal war. The parts of you that were pulling in different directions start to work together. The energy you spent managing different versions of yourself becomes available for actually living.

You stop feeling like you're playing a role and start feeling like you're just being yourself.

And "yourself" turns out to be *enough*.

The Mantra

You weren't made in parts. You were made whole.

Say it until you believe it. Say it until your body believes it.

The fragments aren't who you are. They're what happened to you. The walls between body, mind, and spirit—those were built by a culture that didn't know any better. You can take them down.

Integration isn't becoming something new. It's returning to something original.

Reflection Questions

1. Where do you feel most fragmented right now? Which version of yourself feels most disconnected from the others?

2. What would it look like to bring your whole self into a context where you've only been bringing fragments?

3. When you ask, "What does my body know that my mind is ignoring?"—what answer comes up?

THE INVITATION

You've regulated your body. You've started rewriting the loops. Now the pieces are coming together—body, mind, and spirit learning to speak the same language again.

This is where transformation starts to feel different. Not like effort. Like alignment. Like parts of you that have been at war are finally sitting down at the same table.

But integration without structure is just a good week. The next chapter is about building the containers that make this sustainable—the rhythms and frameworks that keep you whole when life tries to fragment you again.

The whole you is ready. And what comes next will teach you how to stay that way.

Continue this practice. Scan for the free daily companion app.

— **F** —

FORM NEW RHYTHMS

Transformation isn't a moment—it's a rhythm on repeat.

Day four was one of the hardest. I'd been feeling better. The first three days of my new practices had been almost magical.

Morning light, coherent breathing, cold shower, shutdown routine. My energy was up. My anxiety was down. The chronic knot in my stomach had loosened for the first time in months. Something was actually working.

I went to bed on night three feeling something I hadn't felt in years: hope. Not the desperate hope of someone clutching at straws. Not some-day-far-away hope that you can't quite fathom. But the quiet hope of someone who has seen a glimpse of what's possible.

And then I woke up on day four with a sense of dread that wrapped around my chest like a fist and squeezed. My breathing was labored.

Nothing had changed externally. Same bedroom. Same practices waiting for me. Same sequence I'd followed the three days before. But the magic was gone. The anxiety was back—maybe worse than before, because now I knew what I was missing. Now I had something to compare it to. My first thought: It didn't work. None of this shit works. You're broken beyond repair.

My second thought: Why bother? Three good days don't mean anything. You'll always end up back here. You always do.

I lay there, staring at the ceiling, feeling the familiar pull toward giving up. Toward admitting defeat. Toward accepting that change wasn't really possible—not for someone like me. The old loops were already spinning: You're the exception. The one it doesn't work for. Something is fundamentally wrong with you that can't be fixed.

Cindy was still asleep. I lay there a while, watching her breathe, grateful she didn't have to carry what I was carrying in that moment.

Then I quietly got up, grabbed my journal, and sat in my recliner. I didn't know what to write. I just knew I needed to get something out of my head before it ate me alive.

One line came:

Integration isn't perfection. It's return.

I stared at it. I don't know where it came from. Maybe from all the theology I'd absorbed over the years finally landing somewhere useful. Maybe from the three good days teaching my body something my mind hadn't caught up to yet. Maybe just desperation dressed up as insight.

But I've thought about those words a thousand times since. They might be the most important thing I've ever written.

I sat there a while longer. Then did the practices anyway. Not because I felt like it—I absolutely did not. Not because the anxiety had lifted—it was still there. But because that one line had shown me a different way to think about what was happening.

The bad day wasn't proof that nothing worked. It was proof that I'm human. And humans don't transform through one breakthrough that changes everything forever. They transform through return. Through showing up again. Through choosing the practice even when the feeling isn't there.

I stepped outside into the morning light. Did my breathing. Took my cold shower—shorter than usual, but I did it. Made my breakfast of eggs and a protein shake instead of carbs.

Day four didn't feel magical like days one through three. It felt like work. Like choosing something I didn't feel.

But by afternoon, something had shifted. Not all the way back to how I'd felt on day three—but better than I would have felt if I'd quit. Better than the spiral that would have happened if I'd stayed in bed, telling myself nothing works.

Day four taught me something day three never could—this works even when it doesn't feel like it's working. Like the meds I took to control my neuralgia—silently leading my nerve disorder into dormancy.

The practices aren't magic spells that only count when accompanied by good feelings. They're investments that compound like interest whether you feel the return immediately or not.

That distinction changed everything.

THE MYTH OF THE BREAKTHROUGH

We're addicted to the moment.

The conference that changes everything. The conversation with a mentor that finally breaks through. Hitting rock bottom—the one experience everyone will talk about at your funeral someday as the turning point that made you who you became.

I chased these moments for years. Caught a few along the way, too. I've walked out of conferences so fired up I called Cindy from the parking lot to tell her everything was about to change. I've finished reading books at 2am certain I'd finally found what I'd been missing. Once, a mentor said something so simple over coffee I felt my whole life reorganize around it.

Three weeks later? Back where I started. Sometimes worse—because now I had evidence that even breakthroughs weren't enough for me.

Here's what I've learned since: the breakthrough didn't fail. It did exactly what breakthroughs do—it opened a door. It showed me what was possible. Gave me a glimpse of who I could become if I ever figured out how to stay there.

But breakthroughs are moments. *And life isn't a moment.*

Life is the thousands of ordinary days on either side of the breakthrough nobody makes movies about. The eighth month of showing up when you don't feel like it. The Tuesday that looks exactly like the Tuesday before it. The unglamorous work of doing the same thing again because you've learned that again is the whole point.

I've had dozens of breakthroughs. Profound ones. Moments of insight that felt like they would change everything forever. Most of them faded within weeks. Sure, the insights were real. But without a rhythm to sustain them, they evaporated. Vanished into thin air.

What actually changed me wasn't any one single moment. It was showing up on day four when the magic was gone. Day fourteen when I wanted to quit. Or day two hundred and forty when I'd forgotten there was ever another way to live. It was the accumulated weight of ordinary returns that finally made the difference.

The Science of Sustainable Change

When you have a breakthrough, your brain floods with dopamine. It's the same chemical that fires when you win something or fall in love—your body's way of saying this matters, pay attention, something just changed.

And in that moment, it feels true. Everything seems possible. You're not just hopeful—you're certain. The fog has lifted. The path is clear. You can't imagine ever going back to the way things were.

But here's what nobody tells you at the conference: your brain can't sustain that state. Within days—sometimes even hours—the chemicals return to baseline. The feeling fades. And most people mistake the fading feeling for proof that nothing actually changed. They think: I don't feel different anymore, so I must not be different. It didn't work.

That's the trap. Breakthroughs are real. But they're not the change itself. They're the invitation. The change is what you do after the chemicals wear off.

That's where Dr. Caroline Leaf's research changed how I think about all of this. Cindy and I have read a lot of her work over the years. She's a cognitive neuroscientist who's spent decades studying how thoughts physically change the brain (and she doesn't pretend the science and the spiritual are separate categories). Her findings are different than you've probably been told. It takes about 63 days of deliberate, repeated practice to rewire a thought pattern. To take something your brain does automatically and replace it with something new.

Sixty-three days. Not the 21-day myth we've thrown around. Real change takes longer because you're not just breaking a habit—you're building new neural architecture.

Brushing your teeth. Putting on a seatbelt. Reaching for your phone when you're bored. You don't decide these things anymore. You just do them. The behavior has been repeated so many times it's become part of how your brain operates.

The same thing can happen with the practices in this book. Morning light. Protein first. Cold shower. Coherent breathing. Loop interruption. All of it can become as automatic as reaching for the toilet paper—but only through repetition. Only through showing up again and again until your brain stops treating it as a choice and starts treating it as just what you do.

This is why rhythm matters more than motivation. Motivation is a feeling. It comes and goes like weather. Rhythm is a structure—it holds whether you feel like it or not.

Why We Quit

Most people quit not because the practice isn't working, but because they expect it to work in ways it won't.

We come to expect linear progress in life. Every day better than the last. Every week an improvement on the one before. We imagine transformation as a steady climb—and when we hit a dip, we assume we've failed.

But transformation doesn't work that way—it's not linear. It's oscillating. You progress, then regress, then progress further, then regress less. The trend is upward, but the path is bumpy. Two steps forward, one step back. Three good weeks, one hard week. This is the pattern of every sustainable change I've ever witnessed—in my own life and in the hundreds of people I've walked through this process.

I track my own patterns now. Looking back over the past few years, I can see the rhythm clearly: weeks of stability punctuated by days of disruption. Overall improvement—but never straight up. Never a clean line from broken to healed. But progress nonetheless.

If I'd expected linear progress, I would have quit a hundred times. Every bump in the road would have felt like proof that nothing was working. Every bad day would have erased the good days in my mind. Have there been seasons when I fell backward? Of course. I'm human (don't let me fool you to believe I haven't had setbacks).

We also expect transformation to feel good. We associate change with motivation, with energy, with the high of fresh start. And when those feelings fade—which they always do—we mistake the absence of feeling good for the presence of failing.

But sustainable change doesn't run on motivation. Motivation is like rocket fuel—powerful for launch, but not designed for the long journey. It burns hot and fast, then it's gone. If you're waiting for motivation to show up before you practice, you'll practice very rarely.

Motivation gets you started. Rhythm keeps you going.

There's a third reason people quit: they design for ideal circumstances, then abandon ship when circumstances become real.

I've seen this pattern over and over. Someone designs an elaborate morning routine based on what they saw an influencer do. Two hours of practices. Journaling, meditation, exercise, cold plunge, reading, visualization. It sounds amazing. It looks inspiring on Instagram.

Then real life happens. The kid gets sick. The work crisis hits. The travel schedule implodes. Suddenly two hours isn't available. And because the whole system was designed as an all-or-nothing package, they do nothing. One disrupted morning becomes a disrupted week becomes "I'll start again Monday" becomes January. (That used to be my story, too.)

The practices in this chapter are designed for real life—not the social media version of life. They're built to survive inevitable disruptions—because if your rhythm can only survive perfect conditions, it won't survive at all.

FREEDOM CONTAINERS

Transformation isn't about never falling. It's about how quickly you return when you do.

That's the counterintuitive truth that changed everything for me:

Structure isn't the opposite of freedom. It's the container that makes freedom possible.

A river without banks is just a swamp. It spreads everywhere and goes nowhere. But give a river banks—give it structure, containment, direction—and it becomes powerful enough to carve canyons.

Your life works the same way. Without structure, your energy diffuses. Your intentions scatter. Your good days don't build on each other because there's nothing connecting them.

Freedom Containers are the banks of your river. They're the rhythms that hold your transformation when your feelings don't.

Here's what goes inside yours.

BUILDING YOUR FREEDOM CONTAINER

COMPONENT 1: ANCHORS

Anchors are your non-negotiable touchpoints—the practices you protect no matter what. They're the minimum viable structure that keeps you tethered to transformation when everything else is in chaos.

Most people try to build too many practices at once. They read a book like this, get excited, and decide to implement everything immediately. Morning routine, evening routine, breathwork, cold exposure, journaling, meditation, new diet—all starting right now. By Wednesday, they're overwhelmed and doing—none of it.

I learned this the hard way. When I finally got serious about building rhythm, I didn't start with a dozen practices. I started with three. One in the morning—light exposure within thirty minutes of waking. One midday—a two-minute breathing reset before my afternoon block. One in the evening—phone on Do Not Disturb by 8pm.

That's it. Three anchors. Everything else was bonus until those three became automatic. These are my minimums. I often do more. But if everything falls apart—travel, illness, crisis—these three things happen regardless. They're my container.

Choosing yours isn't complicated. Start by deciding what helps you most. What can you actually do when everything's falling apart? I chose morning light because nothing else works if my circadian rhythm is off. By the middle of the day, I flat out know I need a reset—or I slowly fade through the afternoon. The phone? Well, that's too easy (and the hardest one for me still). I refuse to surrender my life to a screen—even though I do battle this one more than I like to admit.

Your three will be different. But write them down somewhere. Tell your partner. Tell your roommate. Tell someone who'll ask you about it. And call you out for lying.

COMPONENT 2: MINIMUMS

Your minimums are the smallest possible version of your practices that still counts. They're what you do when you can't do the full thing.

This is crucial because perfectionism is the enemy of rhythm. When you believe a practice only counts if done perfectly—full duration, ideal conditions, complete focus—you'll skip it entirely on days when perfect isn't possible. I try to live by a principle one of my coaches taught me: Focus. Follow through. Finish. I even printed it and taped it to the wall in my office. It's a good reminder. But sometimes it only adds to the pressure I put on myself. So I also try to remember this mantra—Something always beats nothing.

Thirty seconds of cold water still counts. Two minutes of breathing before a meeting is better than skipping it because I don't have twenty. Even standing by the window with my coffee beats staying in the dark because I can't get outside when it's snowing.

My full morning light protocol is fifteen minutes outside. My minimum? Sixty seconds of light through a window while the coffee brews. My full cold protocol is ninety seconds under cold water. My minimum? Fifteen seconds at the end of a regular shower. I could go on, but you get the idea.

Define your minimums now. When the crisis hits—and it will—you won't have bandwidth to calculate. You need to know in advance what "good enough" looks like.

COMPONENT 3: THE 48-HOUR RULE

One day off is normal. Two days off is a warning light. This is the simplest rhythm-protection tool I've found. If you miss a practice for two consecutive days, you don't beat yourself up— but you do pause and investigate.

One day off requires nothing but grace. Life happens. You're human. Just return tomorrow.

Two days off requires attention. Not shame—attention. Something is happening that could become a slide if you don't catch it.

Here's why: missing one day has minimal impact on the neural pathway you're building. The habit is still strong. The groove is still there. But two days starts to weaken it. A week, and you're essentially starting over. From scratch.

The 48-Hour Rule catches drift before it becomes collapse. When the trigger fires, don't spiral. Just ask: What happened? Was it a one-time situation or something systemic? What's my minimum for today?

Then return. No drama. No fresh start needed. Just return.

COMPONENT 4: EVIDENCE TRACKING

Your brain lies to you. It's wired to notice what's wrong, what's threatening, what's failing. The ancestors who spotted the predator survived. The ones who sat around feeling good about their progress became Purina Lion Chow. So your brain defaults to danger. And it will tell you nothing is changing even when it is.

I know this because I lived it. Three months into my practices, I had a week where everything felt like it was falling apart. Old anxiety. Old loops. Old everything. I was ready to conclude I'd wasted my time—again. I wondered if the whole thing was a mirage.

Then I asked myself a simple question: What's actually different from six months ago?

I couldn't answer off the top of my head. So I looked back at the notes I'd been keeping in my journal—just one line-a-day, nothing elaborate. And there it was. I noticed twenty-three good days in a row with dozens of small wins catalogued in my handwriting. I found conversations I'd handled differently and moments I'd caught myself before I spiraled out of control.

The three hard days were real. But they weren't the whole story. My brain just wanted me to think they were. Now, when my brain starts lying to me again, I tell it to shut the hell up because I've got written proof.

COMPONENT 5: PLANNED DEVIATION

Even transformation deserves a day or two off.

Here's the irony of my life: I'm a pastor. So I work on Sundays. For over thirty years, I've helped other people honor the Sabbath while spending mine on stage pouring out whatever I had left. The day of rest I was supposed to take was my hardest and longest work day of the week.

So I had to find a different day. Like many pastors, Mondays became my Sabbath—not because it's holy, but because it's when I had nothing left to give. I gave myself permission to sleep in if my body needs it. Go ahead and skip the cold shower (or no shower at all). Journaling? I made it optional as well. Did I abandon my practices? Nope. I just held them a little looser.

The real point is that I planned for it. I chose Monday to build rest into my rhythms instead of waiting for my body to force it on me. And since I started doing that, the unplanned crashes don't happen as often. Turns out I wasn't undisciplined. I was just running without a pressure valve. So find your day. It doesn't have to be Sunday. It just has to be intentional.

People Who Found Their Rhythm

Picture a high-level entrepreneur who has purchased every productivity system imaginable. I've met dozens of them over the years. And I've done it myself. Phone full of apps on top of apps. A different morning routine every week (depending on which podcast he listened to the night before). Notion templates half-finished. A cemetery full of habit trackers that lasted three days each—max. Always optimizing and tweaking but never sticking with anything long enough to know if it works.

"I'm searching for the perfect system," he'd probably say. "Once I find it, I'll be consistent."

But he's got it backwards. And I know—because I was him for a very long time. I thought the problem was the system I was using. If I could just find the right apps and combo of routines, everything would click. So I kept searching. Kept starting over. Kept believing the next thing would be the thing.

Rhythm for someone like this (like me) means stripping everything down. Three anchors. Morning light, midday movement, evening shutdown. No apps. No tracking systems. No elaborate process. Just the three things, for three months—with no changes.

The first month, he'd hate it. Too simple. Surely transformation requires more sophistication than standing outside soaking up vitamin D through your eyeballs for ten minutes?

But he keeps going. By month two, he stops thinking about whether to do them. By month three, he's flying on autopilot. He's not deciding anymore—he's just doing. And because he's not burning mental energy on his morning routine, he has capacity for everything else.

"I spent years searching for the perfect system," he might say later. "Turns out the perfect system was any system I actually stuck with."

Now picture a mother of young twins who's convinced rhythm is impossible for her. I've talked with lots of women like this—exhausted, running on fumes, feeling like failures because they can't maintain the kind of routines they read about in books written by people who clearly don't have toddlers.

"You don't understand," she might say. "I have zero control over my schedule. The babies decide everything. I can't even go pee alone."

She's right about timing. Babies don't respect schedules. But she's wrong that rhythm is impossible.

Rhythm for someone like this means trigger-based anchors instead of time-based ones. Not when she wakes up—but the first thing she does after waking, whenever that is. Not when she has quiet—but what she does the moment quiet shows up, even if it only lasts ninety seconds.

First waking moment: sixty seconds of sunlight with her coffee and baby on hip if necessary. First quiet moment: six coherent breaths, however long she gets before someone needs a fresh diaper. First moment the babies sleep at night: phone charging in the kitchen, not the bedroom.

It takes a few weeks to find what works. Some anchors stick, others don't. But slowly, she builds something that bends without breaking.

"I stopped fighting for the schedule I didn't have," she might say after a few months, "and started using the schedule I did have. Turns out I had more control than I thought—just not where I was looking for it."

Now picture a consultant who spends 200 days a year in hotels and airports. Different city every week. Different time zone. Different bed. He's the guy eating room service at 10pm because his flight got delayed... again (this is how I lived for years.)

"Routine is a fantasy for me," he'd say. "I'm never in the same place twice. I'll get healthy when things slow down."

But things never slow down. That's the lie high-performers tell themselves—I did. Rhythm for someone like this means portable practices. Practices that don't require a location.

Five minutes of coherent breathing before checking email—works in a hotel room, an airport lounge, or a rental car. Cold water on face in any bathroom—takes thirty seconds whether you're in Chicago or Singapore. Three written sentences about what went well—ninety seconds in the notes app on your phone.

The insight is separating the practice from the place. He'd always thought transformation required being home, having his environment controlled. But his environment is never controlled. So he learns to carry the rhythm with him.

Six months in, something shifts. He's still traveling 200 days a year, but he's not the same person on those trips.

"The rhythm is in me now," he might say. "Tokyo or Toledo—doesn't matter. The practices are the same. That's freedom I didn't know I could have."

Now picture a recovering perfectionist who has abandoned every personal development program she's ever started. She's got a shelf full of half-read books and a journal full of abandoned goals. Her pattern is always the same: start strong, miss a day, decide she's failed, quit entirely.

"I don't know what's wrong with me," she might say. "I can't stick with anything. I always quit."

There's nothing wrong with her. She just learned some-where along the way that anything less than perfect is failure. So one missed day becomes proof of fundamental inadequacy. And quitting feels better than failing slowly.

The 48-Hour Rule changes everything for someone like this.

"You mean I can miss a day and not start over?"

Yes. One day is just—one day. It's not failure. Two days should get your attention though. But you don't start over. *You return.*

So the first time she misses a day, she prepares for the shame spiral. It doesn't come. The rule is clear—one day off is normal. Return tomorrow.

She returns. And keeps returning. Week after week.

"I've never done anything consistently for this long," she might say at month four. "Not exercise. Not journaling. Noth-ing. I always quit. This gave me permission to be human. And apparently being human is what I needed to actually change."

The Spiritual Dimension

Grace isn't the absence of failure. It's the invitation to return.

Every great spiritual tradition understands this. Confession and absolution. Repentance and renewal. Falling and getting back up. It's death then resurrection. The path isn't about per-fection—it's about coming home again and again.

The prodigal son didn't get it right the first time. He wandered and squandered. He ended up in a pig pen, broke and broken and covered in shame and shit.

But the story doesn't end there. He came to himself. He returned. And the father ran to meet him—not with "I told you so" but with a robe and a ring and a plate of beef roast. I've preached on this passage many times over the years, and the thing that still gets me is what the father didn't do. He didn't make the kid grovel. Didn't put him on probation. Didn't say "let's see how you do for the next six months." He just threw a party. The son who got wasted and had wasted everything was home. And that was enough.

I think about that story a lot when I'm tempted to beat myself up for drifting. Because I used to approach my own growth like a taskmaster. Every slip was evidence of my weakness. Every drift was proof I didn't really want it. I beat myself up for being human, as if being human were a character flaw I should have overcome.

Now I try to approach it like that father. When I drift—and I still do—I don't make myself beg to get back in. I just come back. I pick up where I left off and keep going. That's it.

And here's what I've learned after a few years of this: the people who actually change aren't the ones who never fall. They're the ones who've gotten really good at coming home. They drift, they notice, they return. Over and over. That's the whole thing. That's what transformation looks like when you strip away someone's expectations. It's not a beautiful upward line. It's a bunch of returns.

DISCIPLINE VS. DEVOTION

There's a difference between discipline and devotion.

Discipline is gritted teeth. Force of will. Making yourself do what you don't want to do because you should. It works—for a while. Until it doesn't. Because it runs on a finite resource. Eventually, the willpower tank runs dry and discipline collapses.

Devotion is different. Devotion is loving what you're doing—not because it always feels good. But because you've connected it to who you're becoming. It's showing up not because you have to, but because this is the person you've decided to be.

I don't do my morning routine because I'm disciplined (I'm not). I do it because I've tasted what life feels like without it. And I never want to go back. I do it because the man I want to be does these things. I do it because I'm devoted to my own transformation.

Discipline asks: Can I make myself do this?

Devotion asks: Is this who I'm becoming?

The question matters. A lot. When you're running on discipline, every missed day is a failure. More evidence that you lack willpower. When you're running on devotion, every missed day is just a day. A momentary gap in an ongoing relationship with yourself. And that feels much better.

Devotion is sustainable in a way discipline never is. Because you're not fighting yourself anymore. You're partnering with yourself.

What Changes

Before you form rhythms, transformation feels fragile. Every good day seems like it could be the last. Every bad day feels like proof that nothing's changed. You're constantly starting over, wondering if this time will stick, bracing for the moment it all falls apart.

You depend on motivation that comes and goes. You need to feel like doing the practice to actually do it. Some days you feel it. Most days you don't. You're at the mercy of your own fluctuating moods.

But after rhythms are established, transformation feels stable. Not because you never have bad days—you do. Because bad days are now dips in an overall trend, not evidence of fundamental failure. They're weather patterns, not climate.

Something shifts after a while. You start trusting yourself in a way you didn't before—not because you've become perfect at this, but because you've seen yourself come back enough times to know you will again. The drift doesn't terrify you like it used to. You've developed a skill you didn't know you needed: the skill of returning.

I remember when this finally clicked for me. About four months in, I had one of those weeks where everything fell apart. The old anxiety came roaring back. The loops were running wild. I wasn't sleeping. Cindy could see it on my face before I said a word.

The old me would have spiraled. Would have decided this was proof that nothing I'd been doing actually worked. I probably would have spent the weekend researching some new program or buying another book, convinced that I just hadn't found the right approach yet.

But something was different this time. I didn't spiral. I just got up the next morning and did my three anchors even though I felt like crap. Did them the day after that, too. I wasn't trying to fix anything or find some new solution—I just kept doing what I'd been doing for the past four months.

And about three days later, I noticed I was okay again. Not perfect, but okay. The anxiety had loosened its grip. I was sleeping better. The thing that really surprised me was how much faster I bounced back compared to all the other times I'd crashed over the years. This time was days, not weeks.

That's when I realized what the rhythm was actually for. It's not a shield that keeps the storms from coming. Storms still come. It's a path home when you're lost in one.

The Mantra

Integration isn't perfection. It's return.

Write it somewhere you'll see it. Say it on the hard days when you want to quit. Say it on the good days so you remember why you keep going.

After decades of beating myself up every time I drifted, I needed something to remind me that drifting isn't failure. Coming back is the whole point.

You will drift. You will miss days. You will wonder if any of this is working. And then you'll return. That's not weakness. That's the practice.

REFLECTION QUESTIONS

1. What rhythms have you started and abandoned? What would it look like to return to one of them—not starting over, just picking up where you left off?

2. What are your three anchors? What are your minimums for each?

3. How do you typically respond when you miss a day? What would change if you treated it as normal instead of failure?

THE INVITATION

You've learned to regulate your body. You've started rewriting the old loops. You've begun putting the pieces back together. Now you're building something that can hold all of it—a container for the change.

Breakthroughs get all the attention. But rhythms are what keep you walking through the doors that breakthroughs open.

The next chapter is about what happens when all of this starts to compound. When safety and story and integration and rhythm stop being separate practices and start becoming who you actually are.

That's the shift. *And you're closer than you think.*

Continue the practice. Scan for the free daily companion app.

— **T** —

TRANSFORM YOUR WORLD

You didn't lose yourself—you returned to truth.

L et me tell you about the moment I knew this was real. It wasn't when the pain finally faded—though that was a blessing beyond words. It wasn't when I could sleep through the night again. It wasn't even when I returned to speaking and leading without collapsing.

It was a random Wednesday. Months after the worst had passed. I was sitting in my recliner, nothing special happening. No crisis. No breakthrough. Just an ordinary moment in an ordinary day.

And I felt it—this quiet, steady presence. This sense of being anchored not in what I was doing, but in who I had become.

I remember looking around the living room, almost confused. Cindy was sitting on the couch. Nothing remarkable happening at all. But something in me had settled in a way I couldn't remember ever feeling before. I wasn't waiting for the next crisis. I wasn't bracing for impact. I wasn't running calculations in my head about what might go wrong.

I was just... there. Present. Whole.

It hit me that I couldn't remember the last time I'd felt anxious. Not that morning. Not the day before. The hum of having to produce for someone's approval—it was gone. I wasn't thinking about building something. Creating something. Nothing. My mind was still. And I hadn't even noticed it happened.

That's when I knew the shift had actually happened. Not because I'd achieved something or reached some milestone. But because the thing I'd been chasing my whole life—peace, presence, the feeling of being okay in my own skin—had become so normal I'd stopped noticing it.

That's what this book has been about. Not giving you more techniques to master, though you've learned some. Not adding more frameworks to your already crowded mind. But showing you the path back to something you lost so long ago you forgot it was ever yours.

The Person I Used to Be

I still remember the first time I realized just how much of myself I'd lost to systems that were never designed for wholeness.

It was three months after my health started to stabilize. The neuralgia attacks were less frequent. The aneurysm hadn't ruptured—a gift I still don't take for granted. I was finally sleeping through most nights. My morning routine had become sacred again: sunlight, movement, protein, actual presence with Cindy before diving into the day.

On paper, I was recovering. The pieces were coming back together. The shift was working.

But there was this haunting question that kept rising in quiet moments—one I couldn't shake no matter how dialed in my rhythms became:

Who am I becoming now? And is this version of me actually... real?

I'd been a pastor. A leader. A guy who could work a room and deliver a message. I'd been respected for my capacity to carry weight and solve problems. Right or wrong, I'd built an identity around being dependable, spiritual, and strong. The guy you called in a crisis.

And suddenly, those roles felt like borrowed clothes that no longer fit. I'd outgrown them—not because I was too big. But because they were too small. Too thin. Too disconnected from the person I'd always been beneath my years of performance.

I remember sitting on the deck one evening a few months into my recovery, watching the sun go down. I'd spent the day doing normal work stuff—a conference call, some emails, nothing stressful. Just regular life starting to come back.

But something felt off, and I couldn't name it at first.

I'd done everything right that day. Said the right things on the call. Made decent decisions. Showed up the way people expected me to show up.

And yet sitting there watching the sky turn orange, I had this nagging sense that I was playing a character I didn't believe in anymore. Like I was reading lines from a script I'd memorized years ago but had outgrown.

I opened my journal to write something, but nothing came. So I just sat there.

And after a while, this question surfaced—not dramatic, just quiet and persistent: What if I stopped trying to fit back into the old life and started building one that actually fits who I am now?

I didn't have an answer. But the question wouldn't leave me alone.

WHAT MY DAY LOOKS LIKE NOW

People ask me all the time what I actually do every day. Not the ideas—the actual practices. So let me walk you through it. (And remember, this is the ideal day—I do miss once in a while.)

I wake up at 5am. Not because I'm disciplined—I'm really not. But because I've learned that those early morning hours before the world starts demanding things from me are sacred. They're mine. And if I don't protect them, they disappear.

First thing: hydrate before caffeinate. I drink a full glass of water (16-24 oz.) before I touch coffee. Sounds simple, but after eight hours of sleep, your body is dehydrated, and that dehydration affects everything—your mood, your energy, your ability to think clearly. I spent years pouring caffeine into a dehydrated system and wondering why I felt anxious by 9am.

Then I read my mission statement, priorities, and goals. It doesn't matter what device I'm using, I have them saved everywhere. My mission reminds me who I'm becoming. My priorities remind me what actually matters. My goals remind me where I'm headed. I read them every single morning because my brain will forget if I let it. The loops will take over if I don't consciously choose a different story.

From my mission, I choose one keyword and set it as my intention for the day. Just one word. Today it might be generosity. Tomorrow it might be creativity or excellence or passion. That word becomes a filter for every decision I make. Because I give attention to my intention. When I'm about to react, I ask myself: Is this consistent with my intention? It's a small thing that changes everything.

Then I write in my gratitude journal. Not a lot—just three or four things I'm grateful for. But I've learned that gratitude isn't just a nice practice. It actually rewires the brain. It trains your mind to look for evidence that life is good, you're supported, things are working out. After years of my brain scanning for threats, I needed to teach it to scan for gifts instead.

After that, I recite the *Four Agreements* from Don Miguel Ruiz. Be impeccable with your word. Don't take anything personally. Don't make assumptions. Always do your best. I've been saying these for years now, and they've become a kind of morning liturgy—a way of setting my posture before I engage with the world.

Then coffee. Then protein—eggs, a shake, something substantial. Not carbs. I learned the hard way that starting the day with sugar and carbs sends my blood sugar on a roller coaster that my nervous system interprets as anxiety. Protein first. Every time.

And then I get outside. Sunshine on my face within the first hour of waking (winter is a bit challenging). This isn't optional for me anymore. The morning light resets my circadian rhythm, tells my body what time it is, and sets up everything else—my energy, my sleep that night, my mood throughout the day. I spent years living under artificial light, wondering why I felt so disconnected from my own body. Turns out I was never giving it the signal it needed to know what time zone it was in.

That's my morning. It takes about an hour. And it's non-negotiable. I know I've shared those practices in previous chapters, but I wanted to reinforce my routine to encourage you to copy mine or create your own.

The Practice That Changed Everything

But here's the thing that really shifted everything. The practice that finally broke the addiction.

When I get to my office, before I turn on my computer, before I send a text, before I read a single email—I sit in stillness for forty-five minutes. *Minimum.*

I know that sounds like a lot. When I tell people this, they look at me like I have three heads. Forty-five minutes? Every day?

Who the hell has time for that? But here's what I've learned: *I don't have time NOT to do it.*

Remember what I said in Chapter 2 about your body being addicted to its emotional states? About your cells craving the chemistry of stress and anxiety because that's what they've known for years? About how your body fights your mind every time you try to change?

Stillness is how I finally broke that addiction.

For decades, my body was wired for stress. It expected cortisol and adrenaline the way an addict expects their fix. And every time I tried to change—every time I tried to think differently, believe differently, be different—my body pulled me back. It created anxiety. It manufactured reasons to worry. It generated thoughts that justified returning to the familiar state of stress.

Those weren't insights. They were withdrawal symptoms.

But something happens when you sit in stillness long enough, consistently enough. Your body starts to learn a new chemistry. Your cells start building receptors for peace instead of anxiety. Your nervous system begins to memorize coherence instead of chaos.

It doesn't happen overnight. For the first few weeks, sitting still felt like torture. My body screamed at me. My mind raced with all the things I should be doing instead. Every cell in my body wanted to get up and produce something—because that's what my body had been trained to crave.

But I kept sitting. Day after day. Five minutes at first. Then ten. Fifteen. Twenty. Eventually, forty-five minutes at a time.

And slowly—so slowly I almost didn't notice—something shifted. The anxiety stopped being my baseline. Peace stopped feeling dangerous. My body started to trust that stillness wasn't a threat.

That's when I realized what had actually happened. I hadn't just changed my thinking. I'd changed my body's chemistry. I'd broken the addiction at the cellular level. I'd finally gotten my mind out of my body—out of the memorized patterns and habitual reactions that had been running my life for decades.

The stillness wasn't just meditation. It was rehabilitation. It was teaching my body a new way to exist. And in that stillness, I began to speak my world into existence—declaring who I was becoming, not who I'd been.

The Evening Wind-Down

The morning sets me up. The evening brings me home.

Around 9:30pm, I start my wind-down routine. Phone already went on Do Not Disturb at 8pm. Whatever didn't get done today will still be there tomorrow, and no email is worth sacrificing my sleep.

For the next thirty minutes, no screens. I know this is hard—it's hard for me too. But the blue light from screens suppresses melatonin, and melatonin is what helps you sleep. I spent years scrolling before bed and wondering why I couldn't fall asleep.

Before I close my eyes, I reflect on my intention from the morning. Did I live into it? Where did I succeed? Where did I drift? No judgment—just observation. I also reflect on the Four Agreements. Was I impeccable with my word today? Did I take things personally that weren't about me? Did I make assumptions? Did I do my best?

Then I do something that might sound strange: I congratulate myself for doing my best. Not for being perfect—I wasn't. But for showing up. For trying. For doing what I could with what I had. After decades of beating myself up for every failure, this small act of self-acknowledgment has been revolutionary.

And finally, I tell myself the story of tomorrow. Not a to-do list—a story. I imagine waking up rested. I imagine moving through my morning practices with ease. I imagine handling whatever challenges come with presence and peace. I speak it like it's already happened.

Then I thank God for abundance and influence, and I go to sleep.

That's it. That's my day. Morning, stillness, evening. Like a creature of habit. It's not complicated. Took me over fifty years to figure out. But it was well worth the wait.

The Systems That Trained Us to Disappear

Here's something I didn't fully understand until I almost broke: most of the systems we grow up in aren't designed to help us become whole people. *They're designed to make us useful.*

Think about it. School trained me to sit still. Follow instructions. Produce work on demand. The kids who couldn't do that got labeled as problems. The ones who could got gold stars and moved on to the next level. Nobody ever asked if we were okay. Nobody wondered what we were feeling or what we actually cared about. The system needed output, and we learned to deliver it.

And work? Same system, different currency. You want to get ahead? Answer emails at midnight. Never take a real vacation. Say yes to everything and never complain about the workload. That's the game. As a spiritual leader in a faith community, I've had a front row seat to watch people destroy themselves for a paycheck or a title or just the approval of a boss who barely knows their name. And here's what kills me—we keep promoting the people who sacrifice the most. We reward burnout then act shocked when they end up in my office, or in a hospital, or worse.

Even church—and I say this as someone who's spent his whole life in ministry—even church can train you to perform. Show up. Serve. Smile. Don't ask too many questions. Don't admit you're struggling. Keep it together for the sake of God. I watched people burn out and blame themselves for not having enough faith, when the truth was the system had extracted everything they had and called it obedience.

But here's what really gets me. After enough years living this way, you don't need anyone else to crack the whip. You do it to yourself. You feel lazy if you rest. Selfish if you have needs. Guilty if you're not producing something for someone. I know because I lived it. I couldn't sit on my own couch without feeling like I should be doing something more useful. Couldn't take a nap without the voice in my head telling me I was wasting time. My worth had gotten so tangled up in my output that I didn't know who I was without something to show for my day.

That's not dedication. That's a prison—and the cruelest part is you're the one who built it.

Look, I'm not saying the systems that shaped us were evil. Most of the people running them weren't trying to hurt anybody. But the systems needed us to produce, so we produced. They needed us to comply, so we complied. They needed us to be available, so we made ourselves available. And somewhere along the way, we stopped asking what we needed. So we adapted. Became whatever each room required.

And after enough years of that, I'm not sure most of us remember who we were before the performance started.

The Profit in Your Pain

Here's the ugly truth nobody talks about—there's money in your dysregulation.

The wellness industry makes billions selling solutions to problems created by the systems we're expected to navigate. The pharmaceutical industry profits from anxiety and depression rates that keep climbing. The productivity industry sells optimization to people who are already running on empty.

Your exhaustion is someone else's revenue stream.

Sad. But true.

When you're dysregulated, you're a better consumer. You impulse buy. You stress eat. You numb with alcohol, screens, shopping. You pay for quick fixes because you don't have the bandwidth for real solutions.

When you're fragmented, you're a better employee. You don't push back. You don't set boundaries. You don't ask whether the demands being placed on you are reasonable. You just perform.

When you're disconnected from yourself, you're easier to influence. You chase goals that aren't yours. You measure success by metrics someone else defined. You spend your life climbing ladders leaning against the wrong walls.

This isn't paranoia. It's profit and loss.

I'd be a hypocrite if I left religious systems out of this conversation. And I'm including my own tradition in what I'm about to say. After thirty-five years in ministry, I've come to realize that we do the same thing other systems do—we just dress it up as Sacred. We tell people God loves them unconditionally. And then we measure their maturity by attendance, tithe, and volunteerism. I'm not indicting all faiths, but let's not pretend we don't need people broken to fill our seats and accomplish our missions.

The systems benefit from your brokenness. *All of them.* They're not designed to make you whole—they're designed to keep you functional enough to be useful. Healthy enough to produce. But never so healthy you start asking hard questions about why you're exhausted all the time.

So yeah, transformation is personal. But it's also resistance. It's refusing to keep feeding systems that were never feeding you back.

People Who Found Their Way Back

I've been a pastor my entire adult life. And for years, I've also guided and coached high-level leaders. Sat with thousands of people in the best and worst moments of their lives. And I've watched some of them make this shift.

I think about the executive who finally admitted the corner office was killing her. The teacher who stopped volunteering for everything and started protecting her mornings. The guy who realized his workaholism wasn't dedication—it was just a socially acceptable way to avoid his life.

I'm not going to give you their stories because they're not mine to tell. But I've seen the shift happen. It's real. And it doesn't require blowing up your life. Sometimes it starts with thirty minutes before the kids wake up. Sometimes it starts with finally saying no to one thing. Sometimes it starts with redesigning your environment.

Here's something I wish someone had told me years ago: *your environment will beat your willpower every single time.*

You can have the strongest intentions in the world. You can read all the books, listen to all the podcasts, attend all the conferences, make all the commitments. But if your environment contradicts your intentions, your environment will win.

I learned this the hard way. After my initial recovery, I tried to go back to the same life—same office, same schedule, same relationships, same demands. I thought I could just be a different person in the same context.

It didn't work. The environment kept dragging me back. The old triggers were everywhere. The systems that had fragmented me were still running, still demanding the old version of me.

So I started redesigning. Not all at once—that would have been overwhelming. But piece by piece. I took the books off my shelf that I'd never actually read, the ones I'd bought to look impressive. I deleted social media apps that left me feeling anxious or comparing myself to people I didn't even know.

I deleted apps and turned off notifications completely. My phone doesn't even ring now unless you're in my favorites list. I got tired of being pulled into everyone else's chaos all day long. The constant buzzing was training me to be reactive. And I needed that to end.

My schedule took a while to figure out. I realized I was doing my best thinking in the morning but wasting those hours on emails. So I flipped it. Creative work happens before lunch now. Meetings and calls get pushed to the afternoon when I've got energy for people but my brain isn't as sharp. And I stopped letting anyone schedule anything before my morning routine is done. I used to feel guilty about that. Now I just call it self-preservation.

Some relationships changed as well. This was the hardest part. Some relationships that had sustained me in survival mode were actually keeping me there. People who needed the old me—the performing me, the always-available me, the never-says-no me.

I didn't cut everyone off. That's not what I'm suggesting. But I got honest about which relationships supported my growth and which ones sucked me dry. I invested more in the people who could hold my changing self, who celebrated my transformation instead of resenting my new boundaries. And I pulled back from the ones who needed me broken to feel okay about themselves.

Some relationships deepened as I changed. Some didn't survive it. I'd be lying if I said that didn't hurt.

The Ripple Effect

Here's something nobody told me about transformation: *it's contagious.*

When you shift, the people around you feel it—even if they can't name what's different. Your regulation creates space for their regulation. Your authenticity gives permission for theirs. Your wholeness models what's possible.

I noticed this first with Cindy. As I became more regulated, she became calmer. She says, "I do better when you do better." Not because I was doing anything for her—just because regulated nervous systems co-regulate. My peace created space for hers.

My team started acting different too. I think they'd been walking on eggshells around me for years and I never saw it. Once I calmed down, they stopped waiting for me to blow up.

Problems got surfaced earlier. People actually pushed back on my ideas sometimes, which never used to happen (I didn't allow it). I was trying to listen more and fix less—Cindy's been telling me for years that not every conversation needs a solution.

Strangers too, weirdly enough. I'd be in line at the grocery store and end up in a real conversation with someone. An Uber driver told me about his divorce once, out of nowhere. I don't fully understand it, but Cindy thinks people can sense when you're not carrying a bunch of stress. They let their guard down because you're not making them nervous. I've seen it happen enough times now that I believe her.

Your transformation isn't just for you. It's for everyone your life touches.

The mom who regulates her nervous system before walking through the door—her kids feel it before she says a word. They relax because she's relaxed. They feel safe because she feels safe.

The leader who integrates his doubts with his certainty— his team stops hiding their own uncertainty. They ask for help. They stop performing confidence they don't feel.

The friend who stops people-pleasing and starts showing up real—her relationships deepen. Some fall away, yes. But the ones that remain are more honest than anything she had before.

This is how culture changes. Not through campaigns or programs. Through presence. Through one transformed person at a time, creating ripples that become waves.

THE SPIRITUAL DIMENSION

There's a moment in the Gospels that captures transformation better than any self-help framework. Jesus encounters a man who's been paralyzed for thirty-eight years, lying by a pool that supposedly has healing powers. And Jesus asks him what seems like an absurd question: "Do you want to get well?"

Of course he wants to get well. He's been lying there for thirty-eight years. What kind of stupid question is that?

But it's the exact right question.

Because after thirty-eight years, the man's entire identity is built around his condition. His relationships, his daily routine, his place in the social order—all of it organized around being the paralyzed man by the pool. Getting well wouldn't just heal his legs. It would dismantle his entire life.

Do you want to get well?

It's the question transformation asks all of us. Because getting well—really well, truly transformed—means giving up the identity you've built around your brokenness. It means stepping into a life you don't know how to navigate yet. It means becoming someone you've never been.

The paralyzed man says yes. And Jesus tells him to pick up his mat and walk.

Notice: he has to carry the mat. The thing he used to lie on. The symbol of his old identity. He doesn't get to leave it behind and pretend it never existed. He carries it with him—transformed from a bed into a testimony.

Your transformation is like that. You carry your story with you. The pain, the patterns, the years of fragmentation—they don't disappear. They become part of what you have to offer. Because you don't transcend your wounds. You integrate them.

What Changes

Before transformation, you live at the mercy of your world. Your mood is set by your inbox. Your energy is determined by your calendar. Your peace is contingent on circumstances you don't control. You're always responding, never initiating. Always defending, never designing.

You depend on motivation that comes and goes. You need external conditions to be right before you can feel right inside. Some days the conditions cooperate. Most days they don't. You're at the mercy of a world you can't control.

After transformation, something fundamental shifts.

You stop waiting for the world to give you permission to be okay. You stop needing circumstances to cooperate before you can access peace. You've built something inside you that holds—regardless of what's happening outside.

I remember when this finally clicked for me. A crisis hit—the kind that would have derailed me before. An unexpected challenge. An urgent demand. The old pull toward reaction mode.

But I didn't react. I assessed. I chose. I responded from centeredness rather than panic.

The crisis was still hard. The challenge still required effort. But I wasn't a different person inside it. I was still me—regulated, integrated, rhythmed. I handled the emergency without becoming an emergency myself.

Honestly, I'd always had this capacity. I just didn't have the practices to access it. I was so busy surviving that I never had the space to become—or just be. Now I do.

And everything is different.

The Resistance Will Come

When you begin living differently, you should expect push-back. Not everyone will celebrate your transformation. Because some people grew accustomed to your unprotected self. Some systems were built on your availability and your willingness to sacrifice yourself. They won't easily adjust to your new boundaries. The systems that benefited from my depletion didn't easily adjust to my regulation.

Here's what I've learned: resistance doesn't mean your boundaries are wrong. It means they're working. Systems don't resist changes that don't matter. If no one pushes back, you probably haven't changed enough.

Some relationships won't survive your transformation. That's a grief to be honored. People who needed the old you—the people-pleasing, boundary-less, always-available you—may not know what to do with the new you. Some will adapt. Some will resent. Some will simply fade.

But some relationships will deepen—the ones that can hold the real you, not just the performing you. The ones that want you well, not just useful. The ones that celebrate your flourishing even when it costs them your constant availability.

And yeah, some opportunities dried up. Speaking gigs that needed me available at all hours. Relationships that only worked when I had no boundaries. I'm not going to pretend that didn't sting. But other things opened up. Opportunities that didn't require me to be depleted to participate. I stopped chasing what was killing me. And eventually, better stuff showed up. Not overnight. But it did.

Here's what I know now that I didn't know then: there's a whole new world out there waiting for the whole new you. You just can't see it yet because you're still standing in the old one.

The Mantra

You weren't made to fit into broken systems.
You were made to transform them.

Say it. Every morning if you have to. On the days when holding the line feels pointless and going back would be easier. Say it until you believe it.

Because when you change, other people notice. They might not say anything, but they feel it. Your kids feel it. Your spouse feels it. The people you work with feel it. You become proof that there's another way to live.

That's not nothing. That might be everything.

Reflection Questions

1. What in your life right now—a place, a relationship, a habit—keeps pulling you back into the old version of yourself? Be specific. Name it.

2. If you could start over and build a life that actually fits who you are now, what would you keep? What would you finally walk away from?

3. The man at the pool had to carry his mat. He didn't get to pretend his past never happened. What would it look like for you to carry yours—not hide it or be ashamed of it—but let it become part of what you have to offer?

The Invitation

If you made it here, something already shifted. Not everything. Not all at once. But enough.

Enough to know you can't unsee what's been revealed. To know you're done with survival. Done pretending. Done wearing the old mask that fit someone else's expectations. That's not you anymore.

You don't need another breakthrough. You've had enough of those. What you need is a baseline—something that holds when life doesn't. You need rhythm, not hype. And you don't need to become someone new. You just need to become you. The real you. The one who's been buried under all that performing and proving and pushing through.

That's who I wrote this book for. Not the version of you that looks good on paper. The version that's honest enough to admit you're tired of pretending.

You didn't lose yourself. You just forgot where you put you.

Welcome home.

Continue the practice. Scan for the free daily companion app.

Conclusion

This book wasn't about giving you more to do. God knows you've tried enough. Worked enough. Pushed enough. White-knuckled your way through enough.

I wrote it to remind you of what you already are beneath all that doing. To offer a map back to the person you were before the world convinced you that person wasn't enough.

Let me name what's happened here, because I don't want you to miss it.

You learned that your body isn't the enemy. *It's the entry point.*

Transformation doesn't start in your head. *It starts in your nervous system.*

And until your body believes you're safe, nothing else can change. I wish someone had told me that thirty years ago. It would have saved me a lot of wasted effort trying to think my way out of a body that was stuck in survival mode.

You learned that your story isn't fixed. Those loops running in your head—the ones that tell you you're not enough, that rest is weakness, that your value depends on your output—you didn't write those. They were installed by systems that needed you compliant, not whole. And now you know how to hear them, name them, and replace them with something true.

You learned that you don't have to fragment yourself anymore. You don't have to leave parts of yourself at the door to fit into rooms that were never designed for the whole you. Body, mind, and spirit aren't separate departments. They're one system. And when they work together, everything changes.

You learned that structure isn't the opposite of freedom— it's what makes freedom possible. Rhythms aren't restrictions. They're the banks of the river that keep you flowing in the right direction. Without them, you flood. You dry up. You lose yourself again.

And you learned that transformation isn't a moment you arrive at and own forever. It's a return. Again and again and again. The bad days don't mean it isn't working. They mean you're human. And humans transform by coming back, not by never drifting.

Remember where we started?

I was standing at the edge of my own pool, unable to get in. Trapped in a body that couldn't find its way forward. Medicated. Foggy. Staring at water I knew how to swim in but couldn't remember how to enter.

That man feels like a stranger now.

Not because the pain was fake. Not because the crisis wasn't real. But because something fundamental shifted between then and now.

I learned that my body wasn't the problem—it was the pathway. I learned that my story wasn't fixed—it was waiting to be rewritten. I learned that my fragmentation wasn't a character flaw—it was a natural response to systems that were never designed for my wholeness.

And I learned that the way forward wasn't through pushing harder. It was through coming home—to my authentic self.

That's what I want for you. Not a perfect life. Not an absence of struggle. But a life you can stay inside. A self you recognize when you look in the mirror. A baseline that holds even when the world shakes.

I'm not going to pretend this is easy.

Living this way takes courage. Not the loud kind that makes for good social media posts. The quiet kind. The kind that shows up at 5am when you don't feel like it. The kind that sets a boundary knowing it might cost you a relationship. The kind that chooses presence over performance when performance is what everyone expects from you.

The world will try to convince you this is optional. A luxury for people with time and privilege. An indulgence rather than a necessity.

Don't believe it.

Your nervous system regulation isn't a hobby—it's the foundation everything else rests on. Your authentic presence isn't selfish—it's the greatest gift you can give the people you love. Your integrated humanity isn't a personal preference—it's what we all desperately need in a world that's fragmenting faster than ever before.

WHAT HAPPENS NEXT

Here's what I've seen happen when people live this way:

They stop yelling at their kids—not because they learned anger management techniques, but because their nervous system isn't on fire anymore.

They stop micromanaging their teams—not because they read a leadership book, but because they're not managing their own anxiety through control.

They stop people-pleasing in relationships—not because they got more assertive, but because they finally found their own ground.

And the people around them feel it. Kids relax. Teams breathe easier. Relationships deepen.

This is how the world changes. Not through campaigns or programs. Through presence. One regulated human at a time.

START WHERE YOU STAND

That's the mantra.

That's the method.

That's the whole damn thing.

You don't need to be further along. You don't need better circumstances. You don't need more information.

You need to start where you stand.

One breath. One boundary. One morning of sunlight before screens. One moment of presence instead of performance.

That's how it begins. That's how it holds. That's how the shift becomes not just something you read about—but something you live.

Your shift has already begun.

And the world will never be the same.

Continue the practice. Scan for the free daily companion app.

THE SHIFT MANIFESTO

This isn't a summary. It's a declaration. Read it when you need to remember who you're becoming. Read it when the old loops start running and you need something stronger to run in their place. Read it out loud when you've drifted and need to find your way back. Let it become the voice that drowns out all the voices that told you to shrink, perform, and disappear.

This is your stake in the ground.

I AM THE SHIFT

I no longer perform for love. I live from it.

I don't need to hustle for my worth.

I don't need to outrun my fear.

I don't need to prove I'm enough.

I remember who I was before I forgot.

And I return to that self, daily.

I don't wait for motivation—I regulate.

I don't chase breakthroughs—I build rhythms.

I don't trust hype—I trust what holds.

My body is not a project.

My mind is not the enemy.

My soul is not a mystery.

They are all connected. They are all sacred.

And I am safe inside them again.

I let go of the systems that trained me to disappear.

I stop giving loyalty to what kept me surviving.

I walk away from performance, pressure, and perfection.

This is not reinvention. It's restoration.

I am not becoming someone else.

I am returning to the truth that never left.

I choose slow over frantic.

Presence over polish.

Return over restart.

I breathe. I ground. I remember.

This is my shift.

From fractured to integrated.

From scattered to whole.

From pretending to being.

I don't need to escape my life.

I am building one I can stay inside.

I am the proof.

I am the place.

I am the shift.

Quick Reference Guide

This isn't a summary. It's a field manual. A daily companion for transformation. This is what you return to when motivation fades and the old loops start running again.

How to Use This Guide

When you're starting fresh: Work through one letter of S.H.I.F.T. per week. Don't rush. Transformation isn't a race—it's a rewiring.

When you're regulated: Use this as your daily checklist. Not to shame yourself for what you missed, but to celebrate what you practiced.

When you've drifted: Open to the Emergency Reset Protocol on the last page. No judgment. Just return.

When you're struggling with a specific issue: Each section addresses different challenges. Anxious and reactive?

Start with S. Stuck in negative self-talk? Go to H. Feeling fragmented? That's I. Can't maintain momentum? See F. Ready to redesign your life? T is waiting.

S — Safety First

The Principle:

Your body must believe before your mind can change.

The Mantra

You don't need motivation. You need regulation.

WHY THIS MATTERS

Your nervous system runs the show. When it's dysregulated, your best intentions collapse. When it's regulated, transformation becomes possible—not through willpower, but through biology. You cannot think your way out of a body that believes it's in danger.

The First 60 Minutes Protocol

The first hour of your day sets the pace for everything that follows. Win this window, and you've tilted the odds in your favor.

- **Hydrate Before Caffeinate**

  Full glass of water before coffee. Your brain is 75% water. After 6-8 hours of sleep, it's running on empty. Caffeine on a dehydrated brain creates anxiety, not alertness.

- **Morning Light Exposure**

  Get actual sunlight on your face within the first hour of waking. Not through a window—outside. Even five minutes. This sets your circadian rhythm, boosts cortisol at the right time (morning, not midnight), and signals to your body that it's time to be awake and alert.

- **Protein First**

  Eggs. A shake. Greek yogurt. Something substantial with protein and fat—not carbs. Carbs spike blood sugar, then crash it. Protein stabilizes energy for hours. This isn't diet advice; it's nervous system support.

- **Movement Before Scrolling**

  Even five minutes. Walk around the block. Do ten squats. Shake your body. Movement signals safety to your nervous system in a way stillness cannot. And for the love of all that's holy—don't pick up your phone first thing. Every notification is someone else's agenda hijacking your morning.

REGULATION PRACTICES

These aren't wellness trends. They're neurological resets. Use them throughout your day whenever you feel the familiar creep of dysregulation.

- **Cold Exposure (30 Seconds)**

  End your shower with 30 seconds of cold water. This isn't torture—it's training. Cold exposure activates the vagus nerve, builds stress resilience, and creates a controlled challenge your nervous system can complete. Over time, your baseline tolerance for discomfort expands.

- **Coherent Breathing (5 Minutes)**

Six seconds in. Six seconds out. Five minutes minimum. This isn't meditation. It's mathematics. At this specific rhythm—approximately five breaths per minute—your heart rate variability optimizes, your blood pressure drops, and your nervous system shifts from sympathetic (fight/flight) to parasympathetic (rest/digest).

HOW TO PRACTICE:

1. Set a timer for 5 minutes

2. Breathe in through your nose for 6 seconds

3. Breathe out through your nose or mouth for 6 seconds

4. Focus on the area around your heart

5. Don't force it—let the rhythm establish naturally

6. If 6 seconds feels too long, start with 4 and build up

- **Physiological Sigh (Instant Reset)**

WHEN YOU NEED REGULATION NOW:

1. Double inhale through your nose (one breath, then a second shorter breath on top)

2. Long, slow exhale through your mouth

This is the fastest way to shift your nervous system state. Use it before difficult conversations, after receiving bad news, when you feel anger rising, or anytime you need to come back to center quickly.

EVENING ANCHOR SEQUENCE

How you end your day determines how you start the next one.

- **Phone On Do Not Disturb by 9pm**
  Not airplane mode—you can still make emergency calls. But the notifications stop. The scrolling stops. The world can wait.

- **No Screens 30 Minutes Before Bed**
  The blue light isn't the real problem—it's the stimulation. Every video, every article, every argument in the comments is asking your nervous system to engage when it should be winding down.

- **Tell Yourself the Story of Tomorrow**
  Before you fall asleep, mentally walk through your next day. Not the problems—the possibilities. Not the obligations—the opportunities. This isn't positive thinking; it's priming your brain to approach tomorrow from creation instead of reaction.

WHEN YOU'RE DYSREGULATED

You'll know the feeling. Heart racing. Thoughts spiraling. Chest tight. The urge to flee, fight, freeze, or fix at all costs.

When it happens—and it will—don't try to think your way out. You can't. Your prefrontal cortex is offline. Instead:

- **Notice**

  Where do you feel it in your body? Chest? Stomach? Throat? Shoulders? Don't try to change it yet. Locate it.

- **Breathe**

  Six seconds in. Six seconds out. Minimum three cycles. More if you need it. This isn't optional—it's how you bring your thinking brain back online.

- **Ground**

  1. Feet flat on the floor (remove your shoes if you can)

  2. Name 5 things you can see

  3. Name 4 things you can touch

  4. Name 3 things you can hear

  This isn't woo-woo. It's neuroscience. Grounding exercises shift attention from internal threat detection to external present-moment awareness.

- **Move**

  Change your physical state. Walk. Shake your hands. Roll your shoulders. Go outside. Your emotional state follows your physical state—not the other way around.

H — Heal the Story

The Principle:

Rewrite the loop. Or it rewrites you.

The Mantra

You're not broken. You're running code you didn't write.

WHY THIS MATTERS

You have scripts running in your head that you never chose. They were installed by parents, culture, trauma, religion, and a thousand small moments that taught you what was safe and what wasn't. These loops feel like truth, but they're just familiar. And familiar isn't the same as accurate.

Loop Management — The Four Steps

STEP 1: HEAR IT — NAME THE LOOP

When you're triggered—when you feel that familiar surge of anxiety, shame, or defensiveness—pause and ask:

"What am I believing right now?"

Write it down. Be specific: "I believe that ___________."

The loop will often sound ridiculous once you see it on paper. That's the point. You're dragging an unconscious assumption into conscious awareness where it can be examined.

- **Common Loops:**

    1. I'm only valuable when I produce

    2. If I rest, I'm failing

    3. My needs don't matter as much as everyone else's

    4. If people really knew me, they'd leave

    5. Something bad is about to happen

    6. I have to hold everything together or it falls apart

    7. I don't deserve good things

STEP 2: SOURCE IT — TRACE THE ORIGIN

Once you've named the loop, trace it backward:

1. When is the earliest I remember believing this?

2. Who or what taught me this was true?

3. How did this belief help me survive at the time?

This isn't blame—it's archaeology. You're not looking for someone to punish; you're looking for understanding. Most loops were survival adaptations that made sense in their original context. The problem is they're still running long after the context has changed.

STEP 3: TEST IT — REALITY CHECK

Now you interrogate the loop:

1. Is this actually true, or does it just *feel* true?

2. What's the evidence for it? Against it?

3. Would I say this to someone I love?

4. What would someone who loves me say about this belief?

5. Is this the voice of wisdom—or the voice of a wounded child trying to stay safe?

Loops survive by avoiding examination. They run in the background, shaping decisions before you're aware you're making them. The act of questioning breaks their automatic power.

STEP 4: REPLACE IT — WRITE NEW CODE

Now you write a replacement. But here's the key: *it has to be believable.*

"I'm worthy of love" might be true, but if your nervous system doesn't buy it, it's just a bumper sticker. The new code has to be specific, grounded, and aimed at the same fear the old loop was trying to address.

OLD LOOP: I'm only valuable when I produce

NEW CODE: *My output is not the measure of my worth*

OLD LOOP: If I rest, I'm failing

NEW CODE: *Rest and recovery aren't laziness—they're requirements*

OLD LOOP: My needs don't matter

NEW CODE: *Meeting my needs makes me more available to others*

OLD LOOP: If people knew the real me, they'd leave

NEW CODE: *The people who matter will stay for the real me*

OLD LOOP: Something bad is about to happen

NEW CODE: *I've survived everything—I can handle what comes*

OLD LOOP: I have to hold everything together

NEW CODE: *I can let things fall without falling apart myself*

OLD LOOP: I don't deserve good things

NEW CODE: *Deserving and receiving aren't linked—I receive anyway*

DAILY LOOP PRACTICE

Morning (3 minutes) Before your feet hit the floor, ask: What loop is already running? Name it. Write it if you can. Then consciously choose a different story for today.

- **Evening (5 minutes)**
  Before bed, review: *Where did I react from old programming today?* No judgment—just notice. The act of noticing weakens the loop's grip.

- **Weekly (15 minutes)**
  Set aside time to ask: What patterns am I seeing? Which loops show up most? These are your priority targets. These are the scripts most urgently needing rewrite.

I — Integrate the Whole

The Principle:

Stop fragmenting yourself to fit broken systems.

The Mantra

You weren't made in parts. You were made whole.

WHY THIS MATTERS

Somewhere along the way, you learned to split yourself. The professional self. The family self. The private self. The acceptable emotions. The hidden ones. You became a collection of presentations rather than a person.

Integration isn't about becoming someone new. It's about letting all of who you are exist in the same room at the same time.

THE STACK

Body → Mind → Spirit (in that order)

This sequence matters. It's not arbitrary. It's how transformation actually works.

Body is the foundation. If you're dysregulated—if your nervous system is in survival mode—you cannot access higher thinking. Your mind races. Your spirit feels distant. Everything feels fragmented because you're trying to build on a foundation that's crumbling.

Mind builds on body. Once regulated, you can actually hear your thoughts. You can examine them, test them, change them. The cognitive work of Loop Management becomes possible because your prefrontal cortex is online.

Spirit rises from both. When body is calm and mind is clear, something else becomes available. Call it presence, connection, transcendence, God, the sacred—whatever word fits your experience. It's not separate from body and mind; it emerges from their integration.

This is why all the positive thinking in the world doesn't work when you're dysregulated. You're trying to build the roof before the foundation is set.

INTEGRATION PRACTICES

BODY CHECK-IN (3X DAILY)

Set alarms—morning, midday, and evening. When they go off:

1. Stop what you're doing

2. Close your eyes

3. Scan from head to feet

4. *Ask:* What is my body telling me right now?

Don't judge it. Don't try to fix it. Just notice.

- Tight shoulders? Notice.
- Clenched jaw? Notice.
- Shallow breathing? Notice.
- Churning stomach? Notice.

The act of noticing begins the process of integration. You're rebuilding the connection between awareness and sensation that chronic stress severs.

COHERENT BREATHING (5-10 MINUTES)

Same practice from the Safety section, but with integration:

- 6 seconds inhale

- 6 seconds exhale

- Place your hand over your heart

- Focus attention on the area around your heart

- Let rhythm establish naturally—don't force it

This practice doesn't just regulate—it integrates. It brings body awareness, breath rhythm, and focused attention into coherent relationship.

THE INTEGRATION QUESTION

Ask daily, as often as needed:

What does my body know that my mind is ignoring?

Your body holds information your conscious mind often dismisses. That knot in your stomach before a meeting isn't anxiety to be overcome—it might be wisdom to be heeded. That exhaustion that won't lift isn't weakness—it might be a boundary trying to establish itself. Integration means trusting this information, even when it's inconvenient.

DAILY STACK REVIEW

At the end of each day, ask three questions:

1. **Body:** Did I move today? Did I rest? Did I fuel well? Did I listen to what my body needed?

2. **Mind:** Did I catch the loops? Did I choose my narrative? Did I make conscious decisions or just react?

3. **Spirit:** Did I make space for stillness? Did I connect to something larger than my tasks and obligations? Did I experience presence, even briefly?

You're not looking for perfection. You're looking for awareness.

F — Form New Rhythms

The Principle

Transformation isn't a moment—it's a rhythm on repeat.

The Mantra

Integration isn't perfection. It's return.

WHY THIS MATTERS

Everyone can change for a day. The question is whether you can sustain it when life gets hard, when motivation disappears, when the novelty wears off and you're left with just the work.

This isn't about willpower. It's about architecture. You need structures that hold you when feelings don't.

FREEDOM CONTAINERS

Structure sounds like the opposite of freedom. But here's what I've learned: the right container doesn't restrict you—it holds you. It creates the conditions where transformation can survive contact with real life.

- **Component 1: Anchors**

  Your non-negotiable touchpoints. The practices you protect no matter what.

  Identify your three daily anchors:

  MORNING: ____
  (Examples: sunlight + water + protein, 10 minutes still-ness, morning pages)

  MIDDAY: ____
  (Examples: coherent breathing before lunch, walk out-side, body check-in)

  EVENING: ____
  (Examples: phone on DND by 9pm, review the day, tell yourself tomorrow's story)

  These aren't aspirational practices—they're your bot-tom line. When everything else falls apart, these remain.

- **Component 2: Minimums**

Life will disrupt your ideal. That's not failure—that's reality. The question is: what's the smallest version that still counts?

FULL PRACTICE: 45-minute stillness practice
MINIMUM VERSION: 10 minutes minimum

FULL PRACTICE: Full morning routine
MINIMUM VERSION: Light + water + protein

FULL PRACTICE: Complete evening wind-down
MINIMUM VERSION: Phone on DND by 9pm

FULL PRACTICE: Hour-long workout
MINIMUM VERSION: 10-minute walk

FULL PRACTICE: Journaling session
MINIMUM VERSION: Three sentences

Your minimum is not your goal. It's your floor. It's what you do when everything conspires against your practice—and you practice anyway.

- **Component 3: The 48-Hour Rule**

If you miss two consecutive days of an anchor practice—investigate. Not with shame. With curiosity.

Ask:

- What happened? Was it a one-time obstacle, or something systemic?
- Did I drift, or did I decide? There's a difference between "I forgot" and "I chose not to."
- What's my minimum for today—right now, in this moment?

Two missed days is a signal, not a sentence. But it requires attention. Catch the drift before it becomes a departure

- **Component 4: Planned Deviation**

Rest is rhythm, not failure.

Schedule breaks before you need them:

- One day a week with no practices beyond the minimum
- One week per quarter of reduced structure
- Permission to take a day off without spiraling into shame

One day off doesn't break the pattern. What breaks the pattern is letting one day become one week become one month because you never decided to return.

WEEKLY DESIGN REVIEW

Every Sunday (or whatever day works for your rhythm), spend 15 minutes asking:

1. **What worked this week?** What practices felt life-giving? What structures held?

2. **What got skipped?** Don't shame yourself—just notice. Patterns reveal priorities.

3. **What needs to change?** Maybe a practice isn't serving you. Maybe a time slot isn't realistic. Adjust the container.

4. **What are my anchors for next week?** Name them specifically. Write them down. Make them concrete.

The goal isn't a perfect week. It's an examined one.

T — TRANSFORM YOUR WORLD

The Principle
Stop reacting to your life—start designing it.

THE MANTRA

You weren't made to fit into broken systems.
You were made to transform them.

WHY THIS MATTERS

Most people who transform eventually lose their transformation. Not because they didn't want it. Not because they didn't work hard enough. But because they changed themselves without changing their environment—and the environment eventually won.

Your context is more powerful than your commitment. You can have the strongest intentions in the world, but if your environment contradicts them, you'll be fighting an uphill battle every day.

TIM'S DAILY RHYTHM

Not prescription—example. Adapt to your life and reality.

Morning (5am)

- Hydrate before caffeinate
- Read mission, priorities, goals
- Choose one keyword as intention for the day
- Gratitude journal—3-4 things, specific, not generic
- Recite the Four Agreements (personal anchor practice)
- Protein + coffee + sunshine—outside when possible

Stillness Practice (before work begins)

- 45 minutes minimum—this is non-negotiable for me
- Before computer. Before texts. Before email.

- Some days this is prayer. Some days it's silence. Some days it's wrestling. All of it counts.

Evening (9pm)

- Phone on Do Not Disturb

- 30 minutes without screens

- Reflect on the daily intention—how did I live it?

- Congratulate yourself for doing your best—even when your best wasn't very good

- Tell yourself the story of tomorrow

- Gratitude for what is, hope for what's coming

ENVIRONMENT AUDIT

Your environment is either supporting who you're becoming or pulling you back to who you were. There's no neutral.

Physical Space

- Does my space support who I'm becoming, or does it anchor me to who I was?

- What in my environment triggers old loops? (clutter, certain objects, visual reminders of past failures)

- What could I add that signals safety and intention? (plants, natural light, meaningful objects)

- What needs to be removed or redesigned?

Digital Environment

- Do my notifications serve me, or control me?

- Does my feed nourish me, or deplete me?

- When I pick up my phone, what happens to my nervous system?

- What digital boundaries would support my transformation?

Schedule

- Does my calendar reflect my priorities, or everyone else's urgency?

- Where is the margin? Where is the rest?

- When do I create? When do I only consume and react?

- What would I remove if I weren't afraid of disappointing people?

Relationships

- Which relationships support my growth?

- Which relationships keep me stuck?

- Am I surrounding myself with regulated people, or am I the only regulated one in chronically dysregulated systems?

- What conversations have I been avoiding?

WHEN RESISTANCE COMES

When you start changing, systems push back. This isn't failure—it's physics. Resistance doesn't mean your boundaries are wrong. It means they're working. Systems resist changes that don't matter. The pushback you receive is evidence that your transformation is real enough to threaten the status quo.

Expect resistance from:

- People who benefited from your dysregulation
- Organizations built on your overextension
- Cultural expectations that reward exhaustion
- Your internalized beliefs about what you owe others

Some relationships won't survive your transformation. This is a grief to be honored, not a failure to be ashamed of. Not everyone can go where you're going. That's not cruelty—it's reality.

Some opportunities will close. Better ones will open. The life that was right for survival you isn't right for integrated you. Let the old containers go.

THE RIPPLE EFFECT

Your transformation isn't just for you.

Regulated nervous systems co-regulate. When you're calm, you give others' nervous systems permission to calm down too. You become a non-anxious presence in anxious environments.

Presence gives permission. When you show up whole, you give others permission to do the same. Your integration becomes an invitation.

Wholeness is contagious. The work you do on yourself ripples outward—to your family, your workplace, your community. You're not just healing yourself; you're healing your corner of the world.

EMERGENCY RESET PROTOCOL

When everything falls apart—and it will—this is your lifeline.

1. **Stop:** You cannot think your way out of a dysregulated state. So stop trying. Stop the frantic problem-solving. Stop the spiral. Just stop.

2. **Breathe:** 6 seconds in. 6 seconds out. Minimum 6 cycles—more if you need it. This is non-negotiable. You're bringing your prefrontal cortex back online.

3. **Ground:**

    - Put your feet flat on the floor
    - Name 5 things you can see
    - Touch 4 different surfaces and notice how they feel
    - Listen for 3 sounds you can hear right now
    - Identify 2 things you can smell
    - Notice 1 taste in your mouth

You're anchoring yourself in present reality, not future fear or past pain.

1. **Move:** Change your physical state. Walk. Shake your hands. Roll your neck. Go outside. Your emotional state follows your physical state.

2. **Minimum:** What's the smallest version of your practice you can do right now? Not the ideal—the minimum. One coherent breath. One body check-in. One moment of presence.

3. **Return:** Say it out loud if you need to: "I didn't fail. I drifted. Now I'm coming back."

Return isn't defeat. It's the whole point.

COMMON QUESTIONS ANSWERED

"I don't have time for all of this."

You don't have to do all of it. Start with one practice from one section. Master that before adding more. The FIRST 60 MINUTES PROTOCOL matters most. If you can only do one thing, make it the morning.

"What if I miss a day?"

Then you missed a day. That's not failure—that's life. THE 48-HOUR RULE exists because missing happens. The question isn't whether you'll drift; it's how quickly you'll return.

"This feels overwhelming."

That's because you're looking at the whole thing instead of the next step. The next step is always the same: regulate. Breathe. Ground. Then ask: what's one small practice I can do today?

"I've tried this kind of thing before and it never sticks."

Because you were trying to change your behavior without changing your nervous system. Or you were changing yourself without changing your environment. Or you expected perfection instead of practicing return. This time, the architecture is different.

"What if my family/spouse/workplace doesn't support this?"

Transformation often meets resistance. That's not a sign you're doing it wrong—it's a sign you're doing it right. Start with what you can control: your mornings, your breathing, your internal narrative. Your regulation will begin to affect others, whether they consciously support you or not.

"How long until I see results?"

You'll notice shifts within days—small moments of unexpected calm, slightly faster recovery from stress, brief flashes of clarity. Sustainable transformation takes months. Complete rewiring takes years. But you'll feel different long before the process is complete.

"What if I'm dealing with trauma?"

This framework supports trauma recovery, but it's not a substitute for professional help. If you have significant trauma, find a therapist trained in somatic or trauma-informed approaches. Use these practices alongside that work, not instead of it.

30-Day Quick Start

If you're unsure where to begin, follow this progression.

Week 1: Safety (Body)

- Implement the First 60 Minutes Protocol
- Practice coherent breathing once daily (5 minutes)
- End showers with 30 seconds cold water
- Phone on DND by 9pm

Week 2: Story (Mind)

- Each morning, ask: "What loop is already running?"
- Each evening, review: "Where did I react from old programming?"
- Identify your top 3 loops and write new code for each

Week 3: Stack (Integration)

- Add 3x daily body check-ins (set alarms)
- Ask the Integration Question daily: "What does my body know that my mind is ignoring?"
- Begin Daily Stack Review each evening

Week 4: Rhythm (Form)

- Define your daily anchors (morning, midday, evening)
- Write your minimums for each anchor
- Conduct your first Weekly Design Review

Ongoing: World (Transform)

- Complete the Environment Audit
- Identify one area of environment for redesign
- Begin applying the Ripple Effect—notice how your regulation affects others

Science and Sources

T he science in this book draws from decades of ground-breaking research in neuroscience, psychology, trauma studies, and the emerging field of interpersonal neurobiology. But it was tested first in my own body before I ever asked you to try it in yours. More than four years of living it and almost two years of writing it down for you.

What follows is a chapter-by-chapter guide to the key researchers whose work shaped this framework. For readers who want to go deeper, these sources will open doors to transformative understanding.

Introduction

The foundation of this book rests on the understanding that transformation must begin with the body, not the mind. This insight emerges from several revolutionary fields of study.

Polyvagal Theory: Dr. Stephen Porges' work on the vagus nerve and autonomic nervous system fundamentally changed our understanding of safety, connection, and human behavior. His books *The Polyvagal Theory* (2011) and *The Pocket Guide to the Polyvagal Theory* (2017) are essential reading for anyone seeking to understand why the body must feel safe before the mind can change. His concept of "neuroception"—the body's unconscious threat-detection system—explains why you can intellectually know you're safe while your body continues responding as if you're in danger.

Trauma and the Body: Dr. Bessel van der Kolk's *The Body Keeps the Score: Brain, Mind, and Body in the Healing of Trauma* (2014) remains the definitive work on how unprocessed stress and trauma are stored in the body. His research demonstrates why "bottom-up" approaches that start with physical regulation often succeed where cognitive interventions alone fail.

Chapter 1: S — Safety First

Circadian Biology and Light Exposure: Dr. Andrew Huberman's research at Stanford University on circadian rhythms and light exposure informs the morning sunlight practice. His work demonstrates how light hitting specialized receptors in the eyes (intrinsically photosensitive retinal ganglion cells) triggers cascades of hormone production affecting mood, metabolism, and emotional regulation. His podcast, *Huberman Lab*, offers accessible summaries of this research.

Cold Exposure and Hormesis: Research on cold exposure and its effects on vagal tone, dopamine, and norepinephrine has been conducted by various researchers. The concept of hormesis—controlled stress that strengthens the system—has been studied extensively in the context of cold water immersion, showing improvements in mood, immune function, and stress resilience. Studies demonstrate increases of 200-300% in norepinephrine from cold water immersion.

Blood Sugar and Emotional Regulation: Research published in the journal *Diabetes Care* demonstrates the connection between blood sugar fluctuations and stress hormone release. Even mild glycemic variability can trigger cortisol and adrenaline responses that affect mood and cognitive function.

Somatic Experiencing: Dr. Peter Levine's Somatic Experiencing approach, detailed in *Waking the Tiger: Healing Trauma* (1997), demonstrates the effectiveness of body-first processing for healing. His work shows how the body can release stored trauma through physical awareness and gentle intervention.

Vagal Tone and the Nervous System: Research from the HeartMath Institute demonstrates how states of hyperarousal and hypoarousal directly impact cognitive function, emotional regulation, and immune response. Their decades of work on heart-brain communication provides the scientific foundation for many of the regulation practices in this chapter.

Chapter 2: H — Heal the Story

Hebbian Learning: Dr. Donald Hebb's foundational principle—"neurons that fire together, wire together"—from his 1949 work *The Organization of Behavior* explains how repeated thoughts create neural pathways that become increasingly automatic over time.

Constructed Emotion: Dr. Lisa Feldman Barrett's revolutionary research on how emotions are constructed rather than hardwired is detailed in *How Emotions Are Made: The Secret Life of the Brain* (2017). Her work reveals that emotions are predictions based on past experience, not automatic reactions—which means they can be reconstructed.

Neuroplasticity and Positive Focus: Dr. Rick Hanson's research on neuroplasticity and the negativity bias is accessible in *Hardwiring Happiness: The New Brain Science of Contentment, Calm, and Confidence* (2013). His "taking in the good" practice—holding positive experiences for 20-30 seconds—helps establish new neural pathways and counterbalance the negativity bias that kept our ancestors safe but keeps modern humans stuck in stress loops.

Interpersonal Neurobiology: Dr. Daniel Siegel's work on interpersonal neurobiology, including *Mindsight: The New Science of Personal Transformation* (2010), explains how mindful awareness creates the "space between stimulus and response" essential for narrative change.

Cellular Memory and Emotional Addiction: Research on how cells build receptors for specific emotional chemicals explains why the body can become "addicted" to familiar emotional states—even destructive ones. This research illuminates why willpower alone often fails: you're not just fighting a mental habit, you're fighting a chemical dependency at the cellular level.

Chapter 3: I — Integrate the Whole

Heart-Brain Communication: The HeartMath Institute has spent over thirty years studying heart-brain communication. Their research shows the heart's electromagnetic field is sixty times greater in amplitude than the brain's and changes based on emotional state. Negative emotions produce chaotic patterns; positive emotions produce coherent ones. Their studies on social coherence show that heart rhythm patterns can influence the nervous systems of people nearby.

Heart Rate Variability: Research on HRV (heart rate variability) as a marker of physiological resilience is extensive. Higher HRV correlates with reduced stress, improved decision-making, and enhanced immune function. Coherent breathing at approximately five breaths per minute has been shown to optimize HRV and activate the parasympathetic nervous system.

The Gut-Brain Axis: Neuroscience has mapped the bidirectional communication pathway between the gastrointestinal system and the brain. The gut contains approximately 500 million neurons (the "second brain") and produces 95% of the body's serotonin. This research explains why digestive health profoundly impacts mental and emotional states.

Vertical Integration: Dr. Dan Siegel's concept of "vertical integration"—the alignment between higher and lower brain functions—explains why the vagus nerve must signal safety before the prefrontal cortex can fully activate. His concept of the "plane of possibility" describes the state where creative solutions and wise perspectives naturally emerge.

CHAPTER 4: F — FORM NEW RHYTHMS

Neuroplasticity and Repetition: Dr. Norman Doidge's pioneering research on neuroplasticity, detailed in *The Brain That Changes Itself* (2007), reveals that neural pathways are formed and strengthened through repetition—not through intensity or insight alone. Integration is about consistent return to aligned practices, not breakthrough moments.

Cognitive Neuroscience: Dr. Caroline Leaf's research on how thoughts physically change the brain indicates it takes approximately 63 days of deliberate, repeated practice to re-wire a thought pattern—significantly longer than the popular 21-day myth.

Tiny Habits: Dr. BJ Fogg's research on habit formation at Stanford, summarized in *Tiny Habits: The Small Changes That Change Everything* (2019), confirms that tiny behaviors performed consistently create stronger neural pathways than ambitious actions attempted occasionally. The brain values frequency over intensity when forming new default patterns.

Rupture and Repair: Dr. Daniel Siegel's work shows that the "rupture and repair" cycle—coming back to centered practices after deviation—when approached with awareness rather than shame, actually strengthens neural integration more effectively than perfect consistency.

CHAPTER 5: T — TRANSFORM YOUR WORLD

Emotional Intelligence: Daniel Goleman's research on emotional intelligence, beginning with his groundbreaking book

Emotional Intelligence: Why It Can Matter More Than IQ (1995), demonstrates that integrated leaders create better outcomes across all metrics of success.

Vulnerability and Leadership: Dr. Brené Brown's research on vulnerability, detailed in *Daring Greatly* (2012), shows that the courage to be seen—fully human rather than partially perfect—creates the deepest trust and influence.

Co-Regulation: Research on co-regulation reveals how one person's nervous system influences another's. Leaders who embody integration create a "regulating presence" that helps those around them feel both safe and energized. This explains the biological basis for why wholeness is contagious.

Neurotheology: Dr. Andrew Newberg's pioneering work in neurotheology has used brain imaging to demonstrate that spiritual practices—whether prayer, meditation, or contemplative movement—create measurable changes in neural activity, particularly in regions associated with attention, sensory processing, and self-awareness. His book *How God Changes Your Brain* (2009) explores these findings.

Purpose and Gene Expression: Dr. Steven Cole's research on "eudaimonic well-being" (living with purpose and meaning) versus "hedonic well-being" (pursuing pleasure) showed that these different approaches to life create distinct gene expression patterns. Purposeful living is associated with reduced inflammation and improved immune function.

Mindfulness and Brain Structure: Dr. Richard Davidson's studies at the University of Wisconsin-Madison on mindfulness meditation show that it increases left prefrontal cortex activity (associated with positive emotions) while decreasing amygdala reactivity (reducing fear response). His book *The Emotional Life of Your Brain* (2012) explores how we can change our emotional style through practice.

FURTHER READING

For those who want to go deeper into the practice of transformation, here are essential works that shaped this book:

FOUNDATIONAL TEXTS

1. van der Kolk, Bessel. *The Body Keeps the Score: Brain, Mind, and Body in the Healing of Trauma.* Viking, 2014.

2. Porges, Stephen. *The Polyvagal Theory: Neurophysiological Foundations of Emotions, Attachment, Communication, and Self-Regulation.* W.W. Norton, 2011.

3. Porges, Stephen. *The Pocket Guide to the Polyvagal Theory: The Transformative Power of Feeling Safe.* W.W. Norton, 2017.

4. Siegel, Daniel J. Mindsight: *The New Science of Personal Transformation.* Bantam, 2010.

5. Barrett, Lisa Feldman. How Emotions Are Made: The Secret Life of the Brain. Houghton Mifflin Harcourt, 2017.

NEUROPLASTICITY AND CHANGE

1. Doidge, Norman. *The Brain That Changes Itself: Stories of Personal Triumph from the Frontiers of Brain Science.* Viking, 2007.

2. Hanson, Rick. Hardwiring Happiness: *The New Brain Science of Contentment, Calm, and Confidence. Harmony,* 2013.

3. Fogg, BJ. *Tiny Habits: The Small Changes That Change Everything.* Houghton Mifflin Harcourt, 2019.

4. Leaf, Caroline. *Switch On Your Brain: The Key to Peak Happiness, Thinking, and Health.* Baker Books, 2013.

TRAUMA AND HEALING

1. Levine, Peter A. *Waking the Tiger: Healing Trauma.* North Atlantic Books, 1997.

2. Dana, Deb. *The Polyvagal Theory in Therapy: Engaging the Rhythm of Regulation.* W.W. Norton, 2018.

LEADERSHIP AND INTEGRATION

1. Goleman, Daniel. *Emotional Intelligence: Why It Can Matter More Than IQ.* Bantam, 1995.

2. Brown, Brené. *Daring Greatly: How the Courage to Be Vulnerable Transforms the Way We Live, Love, Parent, and Lead.* Gotham Books, 2012.

SCIENCE AND SPIRIT

1. Newberg, Andrew, and Mark Robert Waldman. *How God Changes Your Brain: Breakthrough Findings from a Leading Neuroscientist.* Ballantine Books, 2009.

2. Davidson, Richard J., and Sharon Begley. *The Emotional Life of Your Brain: How Its Unique Patterns Affect the Way You Think, Feel, and Live—and How You Can Change Them.* Hudson Street Press, 2012.

A NOTE ON SOURCES: This book synthesizes research from multiple fields into a practical framework for transformation. While I've aimed to represent these researchers' work accurately, any errors in interpretation are my own. The science continues to evolve, and I encourage readers to explore these original sources for the full depth and nuance of each researcher's contributions.

About the Author

Timothy Eldred has spent over three decades helping people transform their lives—not by giving them more information, but by showing them how to become who they actually are.

His journey to writing this book wasn't academic. It was visceral. After a life-threatening health crisis—glossopharyngeal neuralgia that sent lightning bolts of pain through his skull, a brain aneurysm discovery that could have ended everything, and a cocktail of medications that left him unable to form coherent sentences—Tim was forced to confront the gap between everything he taught and everything he actually practiced.

The techniques that worked for others weren't working for him. The advice he'd given thousands of people rang hollow. Something had to change. Not his information—his foundation.

What emerged from that crisis became the S.H.I.F.T. framework: a science-backed, spiritually-grounded approach to transformation that starts where most approaches end—with the body.

Because you can't change your life from the neck up.

Tim is the founder of 1:1 Solutions Group, where he works with high-capacity leaders who are successful on paper but struggling beneath the surface. He's sat across from executives, entrepreneurs, faith leaders, and world-changers—and discovered that the most capable people often carry the heaviest hidden burdens.

He's also the author of *Alone Sucks: God's Cure for Our Human Crisis* and host of the *Square Peg Round Hole*™ podcast—a community for people tired of contorting themselves to fit into spaces that were never designed for them.

Tim lives in Michigan with his wife Cindy, who has been his partner in every sense for over thirty-five years. They have two adult children who continue to teach him that transformation is never finished—it's just beginning.

When he's not writing or coaching, you might find him on his back porch, pipe in hand, bourbon nearby, watching another sunset and marveling that he's still here to see it.

Tim believes the world doesn't need more information about change. It needs more people who have actually changed. This book is his invitation for you to become one of them.

LEARN MORE: timothyeldred.com | theshiftplan.com

A Final Word

You made it to the end. That tells me something about you. You're not just curious—you're committed. You're not just tired of the way things are—you're ready for something different. So here's what I want you to remember:

The shift isn't out there. It's not in the next book, the next program, the next breakthrough. It's not waiting for you to get your act together or find more willpower or finally become the person you think you're supposed to be.

The shift is in you.

It's in the next breath you take consciously. It's in the loop you name instead of obey. It's in the moment you listen to your body instead of override it. It's in the practice you return to after you've drifted. It's in the life you design instead of endure.

You don't need to become someone new. You need to come home to who you've always been beneath the noise, the loops, the fragmentation, and the systems that were never designed for your wholeness. That homecoming starts now. One breath. One choice. One return at a time. The shift is yours.

And it always was.